ZEN | FLOWERS

HARUMI NISHI

ZEN | FLOWERS
contemplation through creativity

photography by james mitchell

aquamarine

This book is dedicated to my mother and father,
who have always loved me.

First published in 2001 by Aquamarine

Aquamarine is an imprint of
Anness Publishing Limited
Hermes House
88–89 Blackfriars Road
London SE1 8HA

© Anness Publishing Limited 2001

Published in the USA by Aquamarine,
Anness Publishing Inc., 27 West 20th Street,
New York, NY 10011

This edition distributed in Canada by Raincoast Books,
9050 Shaughnessy Street, Vancouver,
British Columbia V6P 6E5

A CIP catalogue record for this book is available from
the British Library

Publisher **Joanna Lorenz**
Managing Editor **Judith Simons**
Executive Editor **Caroline Davison**
Designer **Lisa Tai**
Photographers **James Mitchell, Norio Asai
and Harumi Nishi**
Stylist **Juliana Leite-Goad**
Editorial reader **Jonathan Marshall**
Production Controller **Ann Childers**

2 3 4 5 6 7 8 9 10

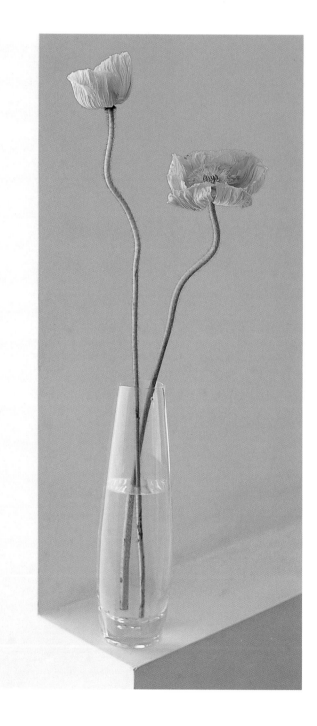

CONTENTS

Foreword

Zen Buddhism teaches that only by contemplating our own inner nature can we achieve enlightenment. It is a philosophy that has greatly influenced the spiritual life and culture of the Japanese people. One of the manifestations of the Japanese spirit is the art of flower arranging *(ikebana),* upon which the influence of Zen has been profound, since flower arranging focuses on the pursuit and development of mental composure. However, my work springs not from Japanese *ikebana,* but from Western flower arranging, as it was here in the West that I studied the art, and it is my objective to blend with creative Western flower arranging the spirit of Japanese Zen. I am trying to create a new approach to floral design and at the same time to instil a sense of tranquillity.

When I make a design using flowers, I concentrate on reaching deeply into my own being; this takes me to a higher plane, freeing me from restraints. In this way, I achieve peace and harmony, my senses are awakened, and I discover a whole new world of values. I try to channel these forces into self-expression: this is where I feel that Zen embraces my art most completely, in the form of creativity that comes from deep within. To discover Zen for yourself in the modern, hectic world is a challenge, since it goes against all the rationality and forms of self-knowledge that you have been taught, but the discovery, once made, is precious and incredible. You see the world as a single entity, like an eternal flower.

In this book, my aim is to show the many facets of Zen flower arranging and floral art; not only the simple aspects of Zen design, but also the other, more complex sides of Zen. Buddhist teaching indicates that meditation is not the only path to enlightenment; we must also seek to achieve it in everyday life, through everything from the creation of art to such simple tasks as cooking and cleaning. It is this philosophy that I apply to the art of flower arranging.

I hope that you will relax while you are reading this book. While I was writing it, being in contact with plants and flowers helped me to learn about the harmony of life, and to see the spectrum of emotions aroused by contact with natural objects. By seeing first-hand the details and processes of plants in their natural form, you too can appreciate more fully the beauty of flowers. Your heart will be taken by their charm. I wrote this book in the hope that each page will calm you just a little, that you will be released from your worldly desires for a moment, and that your body will be suffused with freshness.

H. Nishi

ZEN
AN INTRODUCTION

In the West, Zen is perhaps the best-known and most influential form of Buddhism. In modern Western society, there is much debate about political, moral and spiritual freedom. This is perhaps why many Western people have turned to Zen Buddhism because, with Zen, a person can achieve individuality and personal understanding. At its simplest level, it teaches us about letting go of the mind and rational being, and becoming free to live with the "no-mind". In essence, it is all about freedom, enlightenment and reality.

KI-SHO-TEN-KETSU

The introduction to this book is based on a rhetorical form, known as *Ki-Sho-Ten-Ketsu*, which pervades Japanese literature. It is based on a Chinese fourfold poetic form, which dates back to at least the 11th century. This is the Chinese quatrain, a four-line stanza in which the lines rhyme alternately: the first with the third and the second with the last. This form, when applied to the composition of poetry, is well known in the English-speaking world, but in Japan, China and Korea it is also used in other forms of composition, from essays to newspaper articles.

An explanation of the meaning of the four Japanese words may help you to understand my aim in this brief introduction to Zen and its influence on my flower designs. *Ki* means "introduction" and *sho* means "development". The word *ten* means "turn", and in both Japanese and English this is a general word, open to interpretation. If the form were applied to music, a Western composer might well translate this term as "variation on the basic theme", or "inversion of the original idea", but, whatever the interpretation, *ten* must lead to *ketsu*, which means "conclusion". The first section introduces the subject,

which is developed in the second. The third part describes another subject, which may at first seem unrelated, but the conclusion brings the different parts together and states the argument of the whole. This classical East Asian literary form requires the reader to make connections between the different topics discussed, just as Zen makes connections between the universe and everything in it.

This form enables me to say something about the origins of Zen (*Ki*), the Japanese adaptation and development of Buddhist philosophy (*Sho*), the significance of flower arranging in Zen (*Ten*) and the practical application of these ideas in daily life (*Ketsu*). I have symbolized each of the four stages with a pair of simple flower designs, for flowers are the means by which I express myself. These arrangements are my own personal interpretation of the four elements of the quatrain. I begin with a dot, which symbolizes "origin", develop through the square, which to me is an incomplete form, then through the circle, which is a complete form, and, finally, reach the empty space within the circle.

The rest of the book is divided into nine chapters, each looking at a different approach to flower arranging. Each of these chapters, and the displays within them, has a specific theme, such as the universe in *Mu*, flower bouquets in *Iki*, the unusual or novel in *Bassara* and displays for meditation in *Satori*. The aim is to present an array of flower arrangements that are to some degree influenced by Zen principles and ideas. There are also chapters on Zen gardens and interiors to give you some understanding of the influences of Zen on the Japanese approach to garden and interior design as well as on the art of floral display.

The lotus (*Nelumbo*) is closely associated with Zen Buddhism.

KI | the origins of zen

According to tradition, Zen Buddhism began when a monk, Shakyamuni Buddha, achieved enlightenment as he sat under a tree. Afterwards, he was to deliver a lecture to an assembly of monks, but instead of giving his usual talk he simply held up a flower. Most of the other monks were mystified by this, as they could not grasp the meaning of his action. Only one monk, Mahakashyapa, understood what Shakyamuni meant: the flower was not separate from the building they sat in or the Earth itself, but it was them. With this, the seeds of Zen were sown. It took root in India over 2,500 years ago, budded in China and finally bore fruit in Japan. In Japan, it blended with many aspects of Japanese culture and the two became inseparable.

During the Kamakura period (1185–1333), Zen ideology caught on in Japanese society and grew very rapidly. At this time, religious ideas and ways of thinking developed vigorously, while the social infrastructure of Japan disintegrated, bringing wars, deprivation and misery. People needed something to take them away from the horrors of their everyday lives. The Zen theme of impermanence (as seen in the great Buddhist literary work of the era, *Tale of the Heike*) appealed to them, as did the other central ideas of Zen – non-attachment and non-movement.

From the time of its introduction, the influence of Zen on Japanese culture has been huge. When it was first transplanted to Japan, the original Zen masters wanted to retain a pure, unchanged Zen ideology, as taught to them by their own masters in China. However, as Zen inevitably became immersed in Japanese culture, it absorbed aspects of it, and this gave it a distinct Japanese flavour. Japanese life and tradition treasure the concepts of space, silence and non-existence. For example, in a *noh* play (a traditional Japanese form of staged drama), the greatest challenge for an actor is to achieve silence, or an absence of movement. In a Japanese teahouse, non-existence is represented by the fact that it is free of clutter. Zen plays a central role in these concepts. Zen taught the Japanese to appreciate that all things, even those that seem opposites, are really the same, such as beauty and ugliness; loud, harsh noises and quiet whispers; or vibrant flowers and barren spaces. Zen also reaffirmed the Japanese people's natural appreciation of silence, peace and stillness. In all things, the guiding force of Zen is the search for inner peace of mind in the midst of the chaos and disorder of the outside world.

previous page **These beautiful star-of-Bethlehem (*Ornithogalum arabicum*) symbolize the origin of Zen by showing how a single flower, or idea, can grow into something much bigger.**

below **Hellebores in a transparent container sit well on this small, rectangular table. The cool green of the flowers represents new life and beginnings.**

The objective of Zen teaching is to help the devotee to achieve enlightenment, which Shakyamuni Buddha discovered deep within himself when he sat beneath a tree for 49 days and searched for "the truth from within". This search for one's own truth and good nature is open to everyone.

In your daily life, you may sometimes be filled with tension; you cannot find peace in your own mind. In this state, you tend to lose sight of yourself, lost in an illusion of constant change and pressure. Through looking at nature, and seeing yourself as part of it, you can find true rest, because Zen is all around you in nature. A simple flower is a perfect example of this; it has a certain peace and tranquillity that you can take into yourself. You can begin to experience your true nature by reaching inward rather than looking outward.

Any act of creation comes from within. In art, elements such as brushes, paints and canvas, and even vases and flowers themselves constitute the tools and materials with which the artist works. However, the creative spirit comes from the inner self and, through flashes of inspiration, the Zen artist, like any other artist, creates existence from non-existence. For a person who practises Zen, normal everyday tasks, as well as the making of pieces of art, can become acts of creation. The Zen artist finds beauty and satisfaction in this creative process. In this way, everything in the universe becomes significant.

right **The fresh colours of these green and white flowers on a layer of banana leaves represent the origins of Zen.**

SHO | the growth of zen

Sho

Once Zen had become firmly established in Japan, its influence permeated every facet of Japanese life and society. It is remarkable how quickly and totally the Zen ideology managed to do this. Perhaps it was because, in its simplest form, Zen helps a person to step back and take a detached view, looking at things from a new perspective. The guiding force of Zen – finding tranquillity and peace of mind within oneself in the midst of chaos and disorder in the world – struck a chord for people in Japan centuries ago, and its influence continues to be felt today.

The basic concepts of Zen influenced the way the Japanese saw the world and interacted with it. The original Zen monks took the central ideas of Zen and applied them to their daily lives. The most significant development came when they began to design their living quarters and gardens in the light of Zen concepts. The Zen view of contemplation and calmness fused with the already implicit Japanese love of simplicity and lack of fuss. In time, this led to the development of the classic Japanese house, garden and flower design, and influenced the design of more everyday things, such as cooking utensils. A traditional Japanese house is very sparse, with simple *shoji* paper screens separating rooms, plain *tatami* straw mats on the floor and basic sliding-door cupboards. Like the classic Japanese garden, the Japanese house is multi-functional, unpretentious and offers a place of peace and harmony with the natural world.

Zen Buddhism also played a defining role in the formation of one of the most important forms of Japanese poetry, the *haiku,* which is still very popular today. This is a 17-syllable verse composed of three lines containing five, seven and five syllables respectively. This short and simple, yet precise, form of poetry describes images and impressions, and often mentions nature or a particular season. The influence of Zen is seen in the need for discipline and restraint in fulfilling the strict rules of the fixed pattern of *haiku*; phrases must be simple, without over-decoration, and with the emphasis on the suggestion of an image rather than an explicit description.

Thus, the basic concepts of Zen have had a profound influence on all aspects of Japanese life, domestic, social, and spiritual. So, how can we, at

previous page **The berries of these nertera plants are small and beautiful; they are ideal for forming different shapes. Here, they represent the spread and growth of Zen ideas in Japan.**

right **Red-hot pokers (*Kniphofia*) and heliconias make a perfect match in this elegant, black, cylindrical vase. The bright orange of these flowers represents the energy of spreading ideas.**

far right **These birds-of-paradise (*Strelitzia*), arranged in a line, provide a suitable design for a rectangular vase. Their spiky shape suggests the explosion of new religious beliefs.**

the beginning of the 21st century with our busy and hectic lives, attain a similar peace of mind and find our true nature – our Zen enlightenment? Perhaps these are misleading and tantalizing questions because it has been said that the more you try to understand Zen, the more it escapes you. Zen defies rationality, or any attempt to make sense of it. Instead, it occurs when you let go of your everyday reality, letting it pass you by and feeling the gentle breeze that is created as it passes. In other words, each person must discover Zen enlightenment in their own way.

The Zen person moves away from conceptions and into the actuality of things in his or her inner life. Through daily experience, you can receive the absolute freedom, the *satori,* or enlightenment, that is within everyone. This *satori* is like a flash of inspiration by which you achieve understanding and creativity. The ancient Zen monks saw this, realizing that Zen cannot be taught by verbal instruction, but must be experienced in real, concrete daily affairs, where the *satori* can grow from within.

This is the significance of the flower that Shakyamuni Buddha held up in his lecture all those centuries ago: that Zen is beyond explanation; any attempt to fit Zen into a rationale, or to try to dictate a method for achieving it, is futile. The way to Zen is through personal feeling: experiencing it for yourself and awakening the scent of your imagination. It is the difference between those who know the path and those who truly walk the path. Many books and scholars will offer allegedly sure-fire methods of achieving Zen but, ultimately, the experience should be personal. Hopefully, the flower designs in this book will help you embark on your own spiritual journey.

TEN | harmony in nature

Ten As with other aspects of Zen, its relationship with nature is one of harmony and mutual understanding. The basis of the Zen attitude to nature comes from its inherent respect for all living beings. The Zen attitude has always been one of reuse, an ongoing cyclical flow of matter and energy. In a sense, the original Zen masters were some of the strongest early advocates of recycling and reusing available resources. They would often use redundant pieces of wood from furniture, or surplus roof-tiles, as decorations for the garden, or pick up fallen leaves and branches to burn on the fire in the house. A great respect for nature and a feeling of continuing the circle of nature have always characterized Zen. Zen gardens themselves are often re-creations of much larger natural scenes, such as mountains or panoramic views. For example, the monks who created the famous Japanese Zen temple

gardens of the Muromachi period (1333–1568) were inspired by seeing green, lush mountains with mists swirling around them.

As a part of the circle of nature, followers of Zen have a twofold relationship with the natural world. They are reliant upon nature for food, sustenance and natural resources, but also realize their responsibilities as its caretakers. As it is well within our capabilities to do so, we should all act for the maintenance and preservation of the natural world.

Flowers, which are part of nature, have an intrinsic link with Zen Buddhism. Just as a follower of Zen is searching for enlightenment, we may sit with flowers and create new designs and expressions with them. Zen has profoundly influenced *ikebana,* the traditional Japanese form of flower arranging, with its simple expression and suggestions of seasons and thoughts.

Flowers themselves have been part of many cultures since ancient times. Embracing the beauty of flowers as part of daily life has helped human civilization to flourish artistically and culturally, and flowers have been used for many purposes, such as for ceremonies, decoration and gifts, while herbs have long been used for medication. Nowadays, flowers are mainly used only in the home and for special occasions. Flowers can be much more than this, and have a lot to offer us to improve our physical and spiritual wellbeing. Flowers, individually or as part of an arrangement, are an expression of perfection, or implied perfection. They are also part of an ongoing process; they go through phases of development, budding, blooming and finally wilting. When you see a single flower or an arrangement, you catch a frozen

previous page **The purple-blue flowers and green leaves of grape hyacinths (*Muscari*) may be arranged in different ways to create striking contrasts in colour and texture. Here, an imperfect square has become a perfect circle.**

right **The fundamental harmony of nature is perfectly apparent to anyone who looks really closely at this beautiful black iris.**

moment in its life, a symbol of natural but fleeting perfection. Then, the flowers continue the cycle of life: going back to the earth, nourishing and nurturing the next generation of plants.

You can use the actual process of flower arranging to unwind and relax, to forget your problems and to look inwards. In other words, it can help to make your life less stressful and more meaningful. Arranging flowers can help to create peace of mind and a state of creativity if you bear in mind the guiding principles of Zen and use the process to achieve a state of harmony and tranquillity. By involving yourself in the activity of arranging and changing the image and tone of the display, you can create a Zen-like atmosphere.

For myself, I express my feelings through flower design, not words. The flowers become my language, and the life of the flower is shared with me, giving me strength and soothing my tired spirit. Even when I do not feel like making an arrangement, I receive strength from flowers just by looking at them. Try looking again at a flower you know well; you will always discover something new about it. This is the impact of Zen, when you realize something you did not know before, when something new and unexpected can be created from looking inwards instead of outwards. One of the central requirements of Zen is that every-thing you do should be done with a sense of love. By putting love and care into flower arranging, you can help to foster an atmosphere of serenity and peace.

left **The delicate balance of this display of agapanthus in a bed of hydrangeas shows the harmony found in nature.**

KETSU | emptiness

Ketsu

The goal of Zen is enlightenment, or *satori*. The person who achieves this has managed to let go of distractions such as intellect and language. The mind cannot be relied upon because it is always in a state of change. Things are learned and forgotten, and opinions change. The "no-mind", unlike the mind, never alters. It is an external source of truth. Attainment of *satori* is a source of great interest and mystery. The experience is chronicled extensively, but explanations of what it is are very rare, though the ancient Japanese Zen masters were more willing to speak of their own experience than their Chinese masters. Often, lectures given by Japanese masters included help for followers who had not achieved *satori*.

Generally, *satori* is referred to as a conscious, shining, luminous experience, when the recipient truly sees reality for the first time. The ancient Zen master Dogen (1200–53) talked of reality shining like "one bright pearl" during his enlightenment experience. At *satori,* the physical and mental body is cast off, and the Zen follower can finally see themselves as they truly are – totally at one with everything around them, the world, themselves and Buddha. People have often confused temporary feelings of exultation or intense joy with *satori,* but these feelings fade over time whereas *satori* is a permanent state of being.

Even within the world of Zen Buddhism, conflicting views on attaining *satori* began to emerge centuries ago, leading to two separate schools of thought. The "Rinzai" or warrior school of Zen, states that *satori* can be achieved by meditation, focusing on one short question or statement. This statement can be anything – it may even be meaningless – but the important thing is that the mind is focused. The

opposing school, the "Soto" Zen school, claims that enlightenment can be achieved only by disciplined and structured meditation for long periods, resulting in a slow, gradual dawning of *satori*.

What is certain is the importance of *zazen*. This is the practice of sitting in silent meditation, usually for hours at a time, to achieve the total emptying of the mind known as *mushin*. Both *zazen* and *mushin* are of central importance, and Zen followers adhere strictly to disciplined schedules to achieve them. Once the two states have been established and a pattern of meditation set up, they serve only as tools to gain enlightenment. Many of the ancient Zen masters required years of silent meditation to reach *satori*.

Modern life is very demanding, and it is difficult for us to make time for extended periods of meditation. Fortunately, it is acknowledged by modern-day Zen

previous page **Sunflower seeds are ideal for creating circular shapes; here they have been used to illustrate the emptiness at the heart of everything.**

below **The colours of these drying seedheads of lotus (*Nelumbo*), which signify the new life that can come from death, look beautiful in a dark wooden bowl.**

advocates that you can meditate while doing simple, everyday tasks. The repetition of everyday tasks can help the mind rid itself of unnecessary clutter, leaving you free to reflect and contemplate. Historically, certain natural objects have helped people to focus their mind to achieve the state of *mushin*. Flowers are a perfect example because of their simple beauty and soothing qualities. The story about Shakyamuni Buddha holding up a flower to explain Zen has already been mentioned. It is also recorded that a disciple of the Zen master Ryoko Yasutani gained his *satori* as he was staring at a flower on a temple altar, when the colour of the flower became "incomparably resplendent".

By focusing your mind on the task of arranging a flower design, you can use flowers as stimuli to help your contemplation and provide you with inspiration. The simple elegance of the flowers, and the thought processes you use while creating a design, can lead your mind away from the problems and distractions of everyday life and turn your thoughts within yourself, emptying your mind and beginning the journey to your own enlightenment. Take the flower that Shakyamuni held up all those centuries ago and reach within, letting the gentle breeze of the simple perfection of the flower wash over you, then gradually come to the realization that you are the flower, and the flower is you.

right **Decorative heel mooi is ideal for expressing contrasts, such as the difference between darkness and enlightenment.**

WABI SABI

ZEN GARDENS

A person who lives a life of austerity, practising an art stripped to the bare essentials, is recognized in the West as being ascetic. In the Zen Buddhism of Japan, this asceticism is lauded and recognized as *wabi.* The Zen artist is unconcerned with the extraneous. In the search for simplicity, nothing is added, but much is left out. That is the *wabi* way. *Wabi sabi* describes an object that has the grace and quiet refinement that comes with age. You can find things that are truly *wabi sabi* anywhere in a Zen garden, which can also provide a perfect setting for many Zen flower arrangements.

creating zen gardens

Ever since Zen came to Japan from China in the 12th century, during the Kamakura period, Buddhist monks have been creating Zen gardens so that they may sit quietly in them, compose their minds, and gaze at things in contemplation. Moss and leaves, stones and water – all the objects in the garden – invite you to sit and look. The more you gaze at them, the more their meaning emerges. Most of the stones in a Zen garden are partly hidden or buried, and this is because they are inviting you to look beneath the surface of what you see. The Zen monk, sitting in contemplation of a garden, is not content with looking at the surface of things. He is trying to penetrate their reality. He seeks to identify with everything and to look deep inside himself, as he searches for the experience of *satori* or enlightenment.

The Zen garden expresses perfectly the spirit of Zen. Reduced to utter simplicity, it is a haven of peace and quiet, consisting largely of rocks arranged in an artfully random way in beds of gravel, carefully raked and usually light in colour. Whatever the size of such a garden, it contains a great deal of meaning, for the moss, rocks, plants and pathways are both natural and symbolic.

Let me try to draw such tranquil Japanese gardens into your busy life, so that their sense of harmony with nature will leaven and perhaps reduce the stress of modern existence. Adapt this concept to your own garden and create a region of peace and quiet with stones, pebbles and moss. If, like many people, you do not have a garden, you can create a miniature version using the same elements. Groups of pebbles and other natural objects, arranged on a wooden platter with a few fresh flowers, such as yellow orchids, will create for you an object of contemplation, a peaceful corner in which you may stop to think about your life for a moment.

Modern artists recognize both the ascetic and the aesthetic values of Zen. For example, the gardens of Tofuku-ji, in Kyoto, were designed in 1938–9 by the famous garden-builder Mirei Shigemori.

left **Chozubachis, hand basins carved from stone, have been set before Shinto shrines for thousands of years for the purpose of purification.**

left **A koan is a philosophical conundrum that cannot be solved by intellectual means alone; for example: "Where is the light of an unlit lamp?" The lesson here is to look beneath the surface of things.**

left **This garden in the Tofuku-ji is so peaceful, it is as if it is inviting you to sit and meditate.**

below **Mirei Shigemori's square, granite slabs, in the northern garden at Tofuku-ji in Kyoto, represent paddy fields and are modernist in design.**

His intention was to express the simplicity of Zen in the Kamakura period by using the abstract constructions of modernist art, which also, of course, makes the striving for simplicity its primary concern. "Form equals function" is a concept easily understood by Japanese artists; it might even be said that they invented it.

There are four gardens at the Hojo, which is one of the main buildings of the Tofuku-ji Temple, and these are laid out to the north, south, east and west of the building. In the southern garden, large stones are used to symbolize islands in a typically modernist style, set against a background of moss-covered sacred mountains. The western garden was constructed in direct contrast with the dry stone southern garden; its style is gentle and undulating, its lines being formed by azalea shrubs and moss. Trimmed in a pattern of squares, these plants are cultivated in imitation of *seiden,* the Chinese style of dividing land into different parts. The grid pattern is repeated in the northern garden, but here it is made up of square-cut stones and moss. This garden faces the Tsuten Bridge and the gorge that is famous as a *sengyokukan* – a valley that looks particularly beautiful in autumn. In the eastern garden, seven cylindrical stones, originally the foundation stones of the Tofuku-ji Temple, are arranged in a bed of moss. These stones represent both the main stars of the constellation of the Great Bear and heaven itself.

From the selection of gardens and flower displays in this chapter, you will hopefully gain a good understanding of the main principles behind the Zen garden and the Japanese art of garden design.

the value of an emptied mind

The Kasuien garden, designed by Hakuyou and completed in 1959, was modelled on that of the Sampo-in Temple in the Daigo-ji complex, but its style is unique in that Hakuyou composed his lawns to represent a *sake* bottle and cup. Most Zen gardens in Kyoto are extremely simple, using materials limited to gravel and moss, and these elements contain symbolic meanings. Hakuyou's design makes use of grass instead of moss and, although his shapes are representative, he seeks the beauty of abstraction. His garden is made to suit the modern architecture that surrounds it. The buildings in the Kasuien complex, constructed in the Sukiya style, are the work of Togo Murano (1891–1984), and reveal the delicate touch for which Murano was famous. The striking purple flowerheads of *Allium giganteum* in the concrete container provide a simple, yet effective, focal point and bring a welcome splash of colour to the garden.

left ***Allium giganteum*** **in a concrete vase.**

right **The Kasuien is a fine example of modern Sukiya architecture, with its pared-down style.**

the perfection of silence

In the southern garden at the Hojo, the designer, Mirei Shigemori, has used rocks to symbolize Elysian islands; they are called Eiju, Horai, Koryo and Hojo, and are laid out from east to west on a *hakkai*, a garden floor made of gravel or sand that is intended to represent the "eight rough seas". This scene is set against a background of five moss-covered mountains, which may be regarded as sacred.

Purple hyacinths placed in vases, which are made of thick bamboo, are set against this typical Zen dry garden bed of carefully raked gravel. (Notice how effectively bamboo can be used as a vase.) Purple is the colour worn by Zen monks who have attained high status because of their dedication and wisdom. A Japanese observer will at once recognize the symbolism of all the different elements in this garden.

The circular joints of these bamboo vases effectively echo the circular ripples raked in the sand of the garden at the Hojo.

co-existence

This miniature Zen garden is quite easy to make and does not require many flowers. On a circular wooden platter, groups of pebbles – some white, some blue – are arranged to form a bed; yellow cymbidium orchids may be laid among the pebbles or arranged in standing positions. Some of the flowers fell accidentally among the pebbles, and since they looked lovely where they were, I left them alone. Sometimes, the designer's judgement is rendered redundant: if things happen to co-exist well together, let them be and give thanks for lucky little accidents because they may be trying to tell you something. However, the overall arrangement of green, yellow and white with these beautiful blue-black pebbles is a favourite of mine, and a matter of pure calculation. The tender petals, set among pebbles that are millions of years old, will create an object of contemplation, enabling you to stop and think about your life for a moment.

Yellow cymbidiums and white and blue-black pebbles co-exist in harmony in this arrangement, making a perfect match. The green moss makes a perfect accent to the design.

zen philosophy

This design is an abstract representation of a *tsukubai,* a tearoom washbasin made of stone, said to have belonged to Mitsukuni Tokugawa (1628–1700), a feudal lord, who was also famous for initiating the compilation of the *Dai-nippon-shi,* or the "Great History of Japan". A lovely object that is truly *wabi sabi,* it lies in the garden of Ryoan-ji, in Kyoto. The Japanese characters mean "I learn only to be contented", and this idea – that he who learns only to be contented is rich in spirit, whereas those who seek only material wealth are poor in spirit – is of critical importance in the philosophy of Zen.

Aspidistra leaves mark the stone rim of the *tsukubai* and white carnations (*Dianthus*) stand for the Japanese characters, bridged and separated by bun moss. Pine represents the water in the basin.

a state of tranquillity

The inspiration for this display, which would look wonderful in an outdoor room, comes from the natural world, hence the use of organic materials such as wood, bark, stones and bamboo. The objective of this arrangement is to create a feeling of unity because in unity there is tranquillity. In order to achieve this, all the vases are made of the same material and only one kind of flower, a purple iris, has been used. The impact of the design also relies on the use of different lengths of flower stem to suggest some variety. Differences are accepted; nothing shouts or argues. This is just the kind of welcoming flower arrangement to set at the entrance to the garden or in an outdoor courtyard. The purple of the irises acknowledges the bluish colour of the stone floor, and the use of dark blue paint as part of the backdrop to the display contributes to this theme. Calm, like any other mood, can be created by the subtle use of colour.

The dark blue background behind this arrangement sets off the wooden vases and is a perfect complement to the paler tones of the purple irises.

the harmony of the sea bed

You can create a miniature Zen garden – such as this sea bed garden – and bring it into your living room. It is possible, using the techniques of flower arranging, to make a mini-garden that suits your living space, a garden small enough even to be placed upon a glass-topped table, but simplicity is the key, and it is best to limit your materials to sand, stones, plants and pieces of coral. When you begin to make this garden, you should, of course, summon an image of the sea bed within your mind, but, at the same time, select plants and varieties of coloured sand to suit the colours of your own room. Air plants (*Tillandsia*) and silver dudleya are a good choice, with purple coral and sand to go with the silver leaves. In order to recreate the beauty of the sea bed and provide the whole composition with an appropriate accent, streaks of green and white sand have also been added.

You will need
- **rectangular glass container**
- **coloured sand in bright purple, dark purple, green and white**
- **3–5 marble stones**
- **pieces of purple coral**
- **scissors**
- **2 silver dudleya**
- **3 air plants (*Tillandsia*)**

1

2

1 Choose a rectangular glass container of sufficient depth and ensure that it is not too big for your glass-topped table, for the table is part of the composition and must not be made to appear unstable. Having established a firm foundation, pour and spread the bright purple sand into the container, creating a pattern of underwater ridges. Then pour the dark purple sand into the remaining spaces, being careful not to mix the sands too much and produce a monotone.

2 Add the green- and white-coloured sands to create a pattern that looks like the sea bed, again being extremely careful not to mix the different colours; otherwise, you will lose the nice clean contrasts and the effect will be lost.

3

3 Choose your own method, of course, but you may find that, as you are adding the different coloured sands, it is a good idea to place the silver dudleya and the air plants in the container between one addition of sand and another. Strategic placing of these plants will help to establish the height of your composition.

4 Place the purple coral and the marble stones in the foreground and background to suit your own taste and finalize the effect.

4

entrance to the universe

If you wish to make a design that symbolizes the stars, you should bear in mind that, in Zen, such designs are circular, the circle being an icon of the heavens. One way of forming this kind of symbolic design is to take a number of wooden balls, or other globular objects, and play around with them until you have an arrangement that pleases you. Here, two plain wooden bowling balls, with the knots and grain of the wood still showing, have been lightly decorated with green currants and pomegranate flowers. Having laid a floor of light gravel and placed upon it a composition of ancient rocks, my favourite blue-black pebbles and a variety of other stones, I have positioned the balls to suggest the movement of the stars and planets in space. The half-open door signifies an entrance to the universe.

Rocks and wooden bowling balls represent the planets in their spheres. The green currants and pomegranate flowers are pushed into natural slits in the wooden balls.

finding a place
to bloom

Even if you are not

in the forefront of a scene,

there must be somewhere

you can bloom.

BI

ZEN INTERIORS

Bi means "beauty", and it is believed by many artists throughout the world that the necessary qualities of beauty are wholeness, harmony and radiance. Many artists also believe that the space in which an object exists is as important as the object itself, for its beauty cannot be appreciated without light and space. Art achieves a kind of stasis; it is to some degree distanced from the observer. This concept of distance is given a name in Japanese art and culture. It is called *ma*. This concept should be borne in mind when displaying Zen flower arrangements indoors.

flowers for the home

The appreciation of a beautiful flower requires that the flower should be distanced from the eye of the beholder. The concept of *ma* and its aesthetic significance in the establishment of balance and calm is recognized in Zen and throughout Japanese culture: *noh* drama, the tea ceremony, and the art of flower arranging all exemplify this quality. In the traditional stage art of *noh*, stillness and silence, calmness and harmony provide the basis for outbursts of dramatic conflict. *Ma* is as necessary to *noh* drama as is silence to Japanese music: silence is a manifestation of *ma*.

In order to illustrate this Zen principle, the following pages show the interior of a modern Japanese house. Although Western influence is evident in these rooms, the emphasis given to space and light, to clean lines, to the textures of natural materials, to the absence of

left **A bowl packed with stems of royal fern (*Osmunda regalis*), backed by an ancient print, is a monotonal design in the style of Zen.**

below left **In the *tokonoma* of a modern house, a camellia design is based upon the square and the flowers are given lots of space.**

clutter, and to the distance allowed between one object and another is distinctively Japanese. The integrity of everything is deeply respected, and the overall effect of this respect is the creation of comfort and tranquillity. Such an atmosphere is considered necessary to any home, for it is not only a place in which to enjoy the company of others, it is also a place in which to unwind and regain your composure.

The living room shown at the top of the opposite page is very modern in style. Its coolness is established by a floor of light grey Italian marble, with Japanese earthen walls, a long white sofa – comfortable but devoid of frills – and a staircase stripped to the bare essentials. The staircase is so light in construction that it seems to fly from one level to another like a butterfly. It is unobtrusive, functional, yet beautiful. The windows look out on a patio that is also light in colour, thus serving to enhance the sense of spaciousness. In such a room, so clean and stylish, yet designed for family relaxation, it is a good idea to make flower

left **These white anthuriums, with their very long stems, suit the sparse interior of a modern Japanese living room.**

below **Simple objects set in a simple design can create a serene atmosphere of quiet calm.**

arrangements informal. Keep the basic designs uncomplicated and use simple colours. When everything else is cool, clean and airy, the effect of green foliage, or other natural forms from the garden, can be amazing.

The traditional *tatami* room is very important because it includes the *tokonoma*, an alcove built into the north wall for the purpose of displaying scrolls, flower arrangements and other art objects. The *tokonoma* is an altar, the spiritual focal point of the house, where prayers are said and offerings made. Traditionally, it consists only of walls, but the one on the opposite page includes a window at ground level, which provides additional light, space and perspective. Everything in the *tatami* room is made of natural materials; even the view from the window reveals plants, rocks and stones, the traditional constituents of a Zen garden. Because this house and this *tokonoma* are so modern, the flower design is based on the square. The idea is to create *ma*, or a sense of distance, proper to both flowers and people.

nourishment of life

Calmness and tranquillity are, of course, important in a bedroom, and eucharis, simple but beautiful flowers, were therefore chosen to make a design that would encourage relaxation. The vases were selected for their pure form, length and elegance, and the way that they show off the long, slender stems of the flowers. The beauty of the flowers is distinctive in a room where everything else has been made with elegant simplicity in mind, and these were chosen for their looks alone. It is important not to select strongly scented flowers for a bedroom because some powerful scents are intrusive and can disturb your sleep.

The green stems of eucharis do not intrude upon this combination of brown and white, which creates a calm atmosphere and symbolizes cleanliness.

the mind
replenished

The bathroom is an important place in a Japanese house because it is here that both bodies and souls can be cleansed after escaping from the stressful round of everyday living. The Japanese are even known to meditate in the bathroom, and I have therefore chosen extremely simple plants set in seashells to induce a sense of underwater tranquillity. How pleasant, after a hard day's work, to lie at the bottom of the ocean and watch the fish glide past. As you do so, fresh thoughts and feelings will arise, as if from the sea bed of your mind, and soon, after a well-deserved rest, you will be ready to start again.

Simple objects and plants, including a pair of seashells dressed with orchids, invite you to relax in the tranquillity at the bottom of the ocean.

stones and islands

Playing with stones is a pleasure, as any child will tell you, and it is fun, sometimes, to choose your stones first and set your flower design around them. This is an easy way to create a miniature garden, on a table or on the floor, in the style of Zen. This table, with its light tan surface, has been dressed with long, rectangular strips of linen, which are deliberately dark in colour. To give the stones and other circular objects impact, so that they provide the principal accent, dark tones were also chosen for the plants. Two separate islands, consisting of bun moss and anthuriums, are bridged with the circular stones, and the design is finished with little bowls containing a lotus seedhead. You may find lovely stones like these in the most unexpected places. As the proverb says: "A stone in a well is not lost." And now, neither are these.

The black linen strip at the centre of the table acts as a "container" for this flower arrangement and contrasts strongly with the decorative white stones.

balancing
monotones

When you are tired and all your energy has disappeared, so that you feel lost, like a dot at the centre of a circle, the only thing to do is rest, for it is useless trying to work when you are drained. As your vitality begins to return, it is a good idea to set yourself a simple task, such as creating a flower design using one or two monotones. This may sound easy, but any mistake in a simple design is a big mistake. From the open mouth of this full and feminine cream vase rise the lovely, long green stems of amaryllis *(Hippeastrum)* blooms, bunched at the top to stress both the upright stems and the cascading petals of the flowers. So far, so simple, and so lovely: cream and green, topped by white and quiet red. This is a beautiful object, but care is needed with its setting, for it must not be spoiled. In contrast with the feminine roundness of the vase, a black cuboid chest stands behind it, topped with a large candle, which complements the red of the flower petals.

The quiet red of the amaryllis *(Hippeastrum)* petals is echoed by the colour of the large candle in the background. A pair of tiny red slippers adds the final touch to a lovely design based on just a few colours.

a monk's hood

With light and space, clean lines and pure form in mind, try making a flower arrangement that is wide and long. This allows plenty of scope for free expression; it is easy to make, and it introduces a mood of calm. This container has fairly deep sides, which have been lined with lisianthus. The purple blooms match the colour of the vase, and their rounded shapes soften the sharp outline nicely. With the foundation of the design thus established, blooms of monkshood (*Aconitum*) fill the remaining space. To preserve the clean lines, all the stems need to be of exactly the same length. To make a contrast with this dark mass, narrow, white, cylindrical vases have been placed in a group, slightly to the side of the main display. The long green stems of steel grass rising from the vases finish off the design beautifully. This kind of design allows you considerable freedom in your choice of colours, textures, shapes and contrasts; it is, therefore, very rewarding to make.

If the central feature of your design is a mass of dark colours, set against it a contrast in shape and tone.

pure form

These blue-black vases have a solid but stylish shape, reminiscent of many Japanese things, including the furnishings of a traditional room and the accessories of the national costume. The stalks of the leaves of *Stromanthe sanguinea* also echo the headgear of a kimono-clad Japanese girl. These leaves are strong, with an almost rubbery texture, and are folded into cup shapes so that the flowers sit inside them. To retain balance and simplicity, only a limited variety of flowers are used. The leaves are dark green, but their edges are pink, so the flower colours are related to pink: orange dahlias, red cockscombs (*Celosia*) and yellow silkweeds (*Asclepias*). The rich colour of the cockscombs is tempered by the neutral orange of the dahlias, and these are set off by the dark green of the *Stromanthe sanguinea* leaves. The light grey pebble base echoes traditional Zen temple garden designs, but this display is best suited to a small space, such as a table top. Judge the size of the tray carefully: you want the vases to look neither crowded nor lost in the space.

You will need
- florist's foam
- knife
- silver-coloured rectangular tray
- light grey pebbles
- 2 rectangular vases
- scissors
- 4 *Stromanthe sanguinea* leaves
- cockscombs (*Celosia*)
- silkweeds (*Asclepias*)
- orange dahlias
- arum lilies (*Zantedeschia*)

1

2

3

4

1 Cut a rectangular block of well-soaked florist's foam to fit inside each vase, and wrap each foam block with two of the *Stromanthe sanguinea* leaves, tucking them into the top of the vase around the foam, with the stems extending horizontally. Set the vases on the tray. Position them so that they are parallel with each other, but do not set them symmetrically, side by side, or the effect will be lost.

2 Assemble the two arrangements simultaneously so that they are identical. Starting from the left-hand side of each vase, place the cockscombs next to each other against the curve of each leaf. It is important to set them within the leaves so that the heads of the flowers rise slightly above the edges.

3 Place the silkweeds next to the cockscombs in order to give a nice variety of shapes, textures and colours.

4 Complete the flower arrangement by placing the orange dahlias in front of the silkweeds so that their colour tempers the rich red of the cockscombs, their mass disguises the lips of the cups and hides the florist's foam, and their bold texture dominates the design. Add an arum lily at the back of the display. Light grey pebbles spread evenly over the tray around the vases provide the finishing touch.

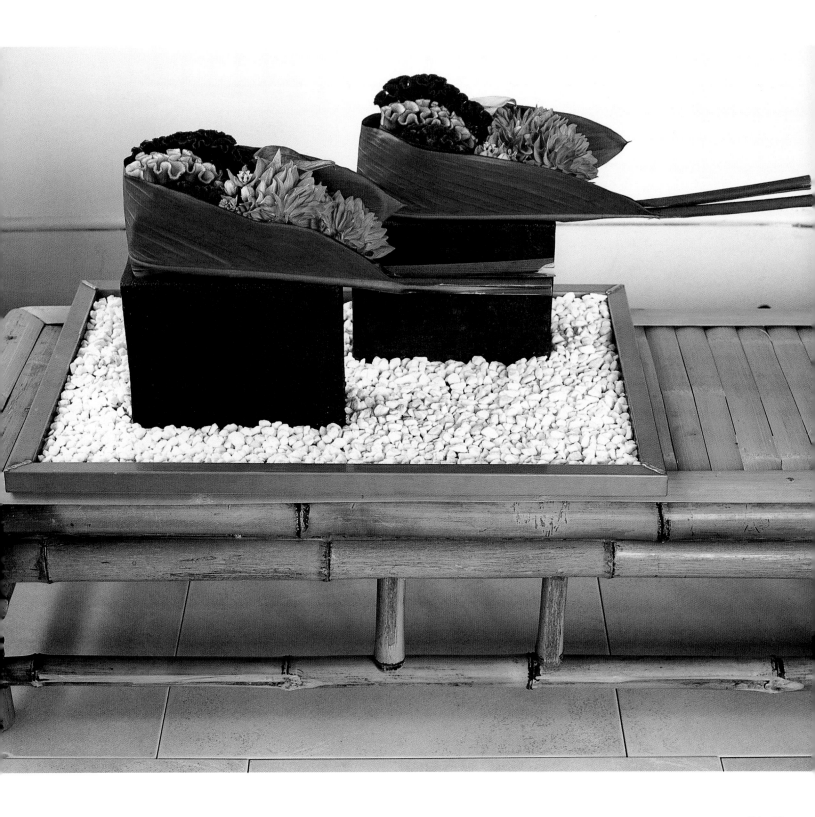

moon flowers

The dominant feature of this design is a metal scroll that resembles the scrolls that hang on the walls of Japanese houses and temples. Because the essence of Zen is simplicity, I have decorated the scroll with a single plant – a monkey cup or tropical pitcher plant (*Nepenthes*) – but it is a most unusual, exotic one, its form suggesting the shape of a saxophone, its colours deep and rich. Leading to this central feature is a rectangular, light brown table, with a broad line of dark pebbles along its centre. These blue-black pebbles are used as a substitute for flowers; to me they signify the trail of beauty. In contrast with these linear forms, the table is set with simple white bowls in dark saucers and each place-setting is dressed with a monkey cup leaf. Although each of the ingredients is modern, the mood of the overall design is very traditional. The final effect is one of simple sophistication.

These simple white bowls, each containing a few succulents, offset the linear emphasis of the arrangement and refer to the moon, an icon of almost every culture in the world.

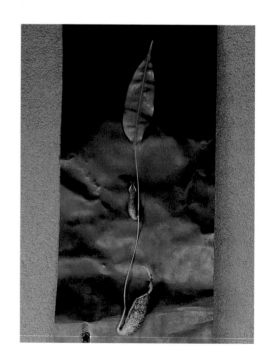

purification

These bouquets of lily-of-the-valley work as a pair and never
display their purity when standing apart, just as people find
it most difficult to discover purity when they are alone.

MU
THE UNIVERSE IN A FLOWER

It is believed in Zen that the entire universe, so complex yet so simple, is contained within a single flower, so it is possible to create a universe within your own home. You can make one or more worlds, depending on your mood. There are many Zen themes on which to base your ideas, one of these being the concept of *mu*, or nothingness, which, translated into aesthetic terms means emptiness or space. In Zen, *mu* is symbolized by the moon.

the beauty of emptiness

A single flower says everything. As it blooms, it liberates the beauty of the universe. It is said that Zen is like a living flower that lasts forever, without beginning or end, its petals falling as new petals grow to take their place. Flowers bloom everywhere – on the mountainside, beside the road, in your garden, in your room and in your heart.

One of the most popular decorative themes in Japan is based on a traditional linear design, and because in flower arranging this theme requires a minimal number of flowers, it is possible to use it in the making of modernist designs. Simplicity is the key. You can use a single flower, or a single bunch of flowers, or limit your flowers to two or three varieties, but whatever you do, the aim is to achieve a minimalist effect by leaving lots of space around the flowers. Artists all over the world understand the importance of space. As they strive to create the wholeness, harmony and radiance of a beautiful object, they know that none of these qualities can be appreciated without the space in which the object exists. In Japan, however, *mu,* or nothingness, is a concept that is not only aesthetic but also religious.

left **A simple vase suits these lovely long-stemmed poppies (*Papaver*).**

below left **Allium blooms and poppy heads shoot from tilting vases like newborn ideas.**

right and far right **This design illustrates reincarnation. The lowest level represents a former life, the middle a present life and the top a future life. The flowers create a connection between the levels.**

When you make Zen flower arrangements, you should strive for perfect simplicity by giving full acknowledgement to everything that is *not* the design.

In strictly practical terms, the easiest way to begin is by making a design with one flower and one vase. First, judge the flower and the length of its stem, then balance both flower and stem with the vase that you have chosen. If you wish to create something in *wabi sabi* mood, cherry blossom or bamboo will set this mood for you, but if you prefer to acknowledge *mu* in a modernist way, it would be better to choose gerbera or orchids, as they have a contemporary look.

In many Japanese Zen gardens, stones are used to represent the universe, and if you wish to create such a space in your home, it is easy to make a tiny Zen garden, using stones and plants as your foundation. It is also great fun to look for the stones, which you can find anywhere: in the road, on the common or in the park. Once you begin to look properly at stones – all of which are millions of years old – it is amazing to see how beautiful they can be.

Finally, if you wish to make a design that illustrates the universe in some way, why not take a ball of florist's foam or moss and decorate it with flower petals? Used as the basis of your design, you can make a number of them to represent planets and stars.

The display on this page is designed to show the continuity of life in the universe. You will need some cuboid containers of glass or clear plastic; you can even use CD boxes. Behind this very interesting design is the idea of reincarnation, and, whether or not you accept this Buddhist concept, I think you will agree with me that it has given rise to a striking

contemporary composition. In this design, I wished to construct three physically separated levels, a lower level representing a former life, a middle level representing a present life and an upper level representing a future life. I then sought to suggest by the use of these gerbera stalks and blooms a connection between the levels that was spiritual in nature, the stalks standing for growth and the blooms for fruition. Of course, this design also reveals the connections between all things in the universe. In purely aesthetic terms, notice how the simple, functional form of the container shows off to such good effect the form and colour of the flower.

In this kind of design, the skill lies in knowing when to stop; it resides in the ability to sense when the wholeness, harmony and radiance of the object is demonstrated, and there is nothing more to be done. Like everything in Zen, this is both simple and difficult, and requires great sensitivity, but when you have managed to achieve the ultimate blending of an object with the space in which it rests, then you have said something about the simplicity and the beauty of the universe. At that moment, you can feel the satisfaction of being in touch with reality – both the great reality outside and the reality within yourself. This moment of satisfaction is one in which the heart is healed.

a diffusion of flowers

When you have mastered the minimalist art of making a complete design with only a single vase and a single flower, surrounded by space and light, then you are ready to appreciate the flower as a single, separate entity. Sometimes, the natural shape of a flower is so suggestive that a word and a flower are almost inseparable in the mind – that is how flowers become symbols. Here, the word is "diffusion", and the scattering of light and fragrance is suggested by the white or purple petals of agapanthus and the petals of papyrus (*Cyperus papyrus*). They are arranged in light and space as a combination of single entities in order to best display their qualities, seductive both to the eye and to the sense of smell. As they diffuse their light and fragrance, so they spread a sense of calm and inner peace; sometimes, the effect of flowers is so hypnotic that you can be sent into a deep, restful slumber.

White agapanthus

Purple agapanthus

Everything seems to move upwards and outwards in these agapanthus and papyrus blooms; they are perfect for a design based on the theme of diffusion. A single stem of eryngium adds a splash of colour.

chrysanthemum galaxy

When I visit the Zen gardens in Kyoto, Japan, and gaze at the stones and rocks in the gravel beds, I imagine them to be half-buried, their ultimate forms hidden. That which is hidden is left to the imagination. There is a trend in modernist design, however, that involves the stripping bare of objects, so that everything is revealed. In keeping with this trend, I have tried to suggest stones and rocks in a Zen garden, but have displayed the objects in their entirety. The chrysanthemum heads also represent souls adrift in the vastness of a universe not as yet fully understood.

Each of the spheres in the display is composed of two hemispheres. These are glued to the bottom of a glass box as well as to the inverted lid. This gives the impression that the spheres are floating.

monte carlo
tulips

In the bathroom you can relax and allow your imagination to roam the universe. If you need something to take your mind off reality, set your fantasy in motion with these miniature reminders of the vastness out there, and dispel all sense of weariness with the vivid yellow tulip 'Monte Carlo'. They cannot fail to cheer you up. The deep green of the glass vases suggests cleansing water as well as space, so you will soon feel free again, refreshed in body and soul. This is an example of the striking effect that can be achieved with a simple vase and a single kind of bloom, set in space and light so that its qualities can be appreciated. Yellow and dark green go together perfectly to suggest freshness and health. The subtle green tones in the tulip blooms echo the overall colour of the vase, and the vase returns the compliment with its streaks of yellow. White walls and glass shelves can be cold and bare until you place something like this upon them.

The yellow of these tulips goes perfectly with the dark green of the vases. Yellow lines in the green glass connect the colours and suggest the swirling masses to be seen in deep space.

a single flower

A single flower can shine like a lone star and illuminate the beauty of the universe. In this design, a large, black dish suggests the dark space of the universe, and within this space a galaxy is made of hydrangea and lotus (*Nelumbo*) seedheads. Within this muted setting, I played with a single flower – a pink poppy (*Papaver*) – until I had made a satisfying design. The whole thing can be seen as a pleasing design, or – if you wish to exercise imagination – as the birth of a star, the light of which shines on the surrounding universe. It is always a good idea to take a single bloom, examine its qualities, decide what you want it to represent and then choose the other elements. In this way, you work from the centre, for the flower establishes your basic theme and simplifies all your decisions. Of course, it is also possible to work the other way round, starting, in this case, with the circular black dish; the important thing is to begin with a clear idea.

On a large wooden dish, the head of a hydrangea, a lotus seedhead and a poppy bloom represent the birth of a star.

the source of zen

Zen has its apparent source in the human mind, conditioned by several thousand years of human history, but its ultimate source – like that of everything else – is the universe, which no one fully understands, and so the true source of Zen is mysterious. The more you understand, the less you know, and the more you think you know, the deeper is your ignorance. Both Zen and the flower spring from the same unfathomable source, and that is the link between them. Whenever I choose a universal theme, I am tempted by the colours blue, purple and grey. Here, the subtle combination of colours of the hydrangea blooms, the plinth and the pale blue background suggests the basic unity of all things within the universe.

These beautiful hydrangea blooms, set on top of a silver plinth and placed in front of a background of impenetrable blue, have become an icon of the universe.

global flowers

When you create designs based upon a conception of the universe, it is a good idea to use flowers whose shapes echo that conception. Since our collective knowledge makes it clear that the universe is an expanding mass, almost everyone sees it as a ball of some kind. Provided that you accept the evidence of scientific investigation and visualize the universe in this way, circular and spherical shapes are very useful in the creation of such designs. A large circular dish immediately establishes the motif of a miniature universe. Likewise, plants with globular heads or masses of petals, such as *Allium sphaerocephalon*, *A. aflatunense*, or *Ornithogalum arabicum*, help to establish and suggest a concept that is practically universal.

You will need
- circular dish
- florist's foam
- florist's tape
- scissors
- *Allium aflatunense*
- *Allium sphaerocephalon*
- *Ornithogalum arabicum*

1

2

1 Having chosen the table on which you will place your arrangement and decorated it as you wish, take a large wooden dish and place it in the centre of the table. Cut several blocks of well-soaked florist's foam, then tape two of the blocks together to give a double thickness which will provide a secure foundation for an *Allium aflatunense* bloom with a long stem. This longer stem will give height to your design. Place some of the smaller *Allium aflatunense* blooms in the bowl, securing the stems horizonally in the florist's foam.

2 To give the design a contemporary appearance, arrange the stems in parallel lines as you add the blooms of *Allium sphaerocephalon* and *Ornithogalum arabicum.*

3 Visualize the effect that the larger heads of the *Allium aflatunense* will have on the arrangement as you position the smaller flowers. Then begin to add the larger blooms, always bearing in mind the final balance of mass and colour in the arrangement.

4 Once you have achieved a nice balance of the various rounded forms of the flowers, and set these off with parallel verticals and horizontals, use the remaining blooms to conceal the florist's foam completely. Complete the design by inserting a long-stemmed bloom of *Allium aflatunense* into the prepared foam base.

3

4

miniature universe

The textures and forms of anthurium blooms and the leaves of the elephant's ear plant (*Alocasia*) are very well suited to modernist designs. Anthuriums are at the same time simple and beautiful, so the satisfying simplicity of this silver-coloured globe makes it just the right sort of object to combine with these unusual flowers. To make such an arrangement as effective as possible, choose your colours carefully. Try to avoid vivid hues, which will have too powerful an effect. As you are dealing with simplicity of line and form, delicacy and subtlety are the key words.

Express the beauty of the universe simply with a few anthuriums.

scent of imagination

A true understanding of reality can
only be achieved through the mind.

IKI
ZEN BOUQUET

Flowers have occupied a special place in Japanese culture since time immemorial. They epitomize *iki,* or stylishness. According to legend, the birth of Shakyamuni Buddha gave rise to an outburst of heavenly birdsong, sweet tea showered from the skies and fragrant flowers of the field descended upon him. This is why, together with candles and incense, fresh flowers are placed upon Buddhist altars.

the art of flower design

The Japanese love affair with nature in general, and with flowers and plants in particular, predates by many years the introduction of Zen Buddhism to Japan in the 12th century. Indeed, it goes so far back into prehistory that no one can possibly say when it began.

Japanese culture is rooted in the earth. The earliest known tribes of the sacred islands were agrarian, and the religion popularly known as Shinto is a religion of nature-worship. A *kami*, or natural spirit, is believed to inhabit everything, from a star in the sky to the humblest insect or even a piece of rock. There is no moral preoccupation with sin in Shinto, and no concept of an afterlife; the object of worship is the universe in which we exist – the universe and all the strange and wonderful things that blossom within it. In a similar way, simple objects in space and light are objects of reverential contemplation in Zen Buddhism. That is why a single flower, in its simplicity and its unfathomable complexity, says all

there is to say. In terms of written history, evidence of the Japanese love of flowers may be found in hundreds of verses penned by the people of Nara when it was the capital of the sacred land in the 8th century. Of the 4,500 verses in the *Manyoshu*, which is an anthology of ancient poems, approximately one-third deal with plants and flowers.

The lotus flower is the basic platform for all images of the Buddha, whether seated or upright, and this platform may be simulated in many different ways. For example, it can be painted or made from metal or paper. The lotus motif is also used for decorative purposes in Buddhist religious imagery. In Buddhist flower arranging, the lotus flower provides a fundamental motif. When a central branch is presented on such a platform, it is used to represent the Buddha. This basic structure is known as *rikka,* which refers to a flower arrangement that is standing or erect. *Rikka* is also echoed in Shinto nature festivals, such as the summer festival

left **Green-flowered plants, including bells-of-Ireland (*Moluccella laevis*) and hellebores as well as an anthurium leaf, stand erect in glass containers.**

right **The green tones of hellebore look wonderful in a wooden dish. The plants seem to arrange themselves.**

ikebana itself embraces many different forms, including the primitive style of *rikka*. *Seika*, another form of *ikebana*, means "cut flowers", and is analogous with *rikka* in that it is highly correct and formal. It is frequently used in Buddhist shrines, or in the living rooms of city-dwellers, but the style reflects the way the flowers appear when they are living. *Nageire*, on the other hand, is the "loose" way of arranging flowers. Although the basic form of the triangle provides the foundation of all these styles, *nageire* is literally translated as "thrown in", and this style is in sharp contrast with the rigid, formal styles of *rikka* and *seika*.

The original practice of *nageire* involved placing the flowers in hanging vases in order to create soft, flowing lines, and this is a style of flower arranging that particularly appeals to me. I have been influenced, whether consciously or unconsciously, by many different styles of flower-arranging, but it is very rewarding to develop your own individual style and approach, and to use flower arranging as a means of expressing and exploring your own thoughts and feelings.

The selection of flower arrangements in this section are particularly stylish and take advantage of the sheer "smartness" of Zen, drawing on its emphasis on light and space, as well as on its preoccupation with clean lines and pure form.

at the Gion shrine in Kyoto, where antique floats are pulled through the streets by celebrating crowds. Each of these floats carries a tall mast, on to which are tied the branches of a sacred tree. This arrangement, which is made as an offering to the *kami*, is the Shinto equivalent of the Buddhist *rikka* arrangement. The Gion festival is known to be at least 700 years old, but such festivals and such symbolic offerings are known to date back to the dawning of Japanese civilization.

From such ancient customs grew the secular art form of flower arranging known as *ikebana*. *Bana* means flower, and *ikebana* the preserving of flowers in water containers, but for the Japanese "flower" is a broad term, which includes any form of plant life. Indeed,

above left and right
These monotone black and white vases make a perfect match with *Delphinium elatum* 'White Arrow'. Notice, too, the matching of shapes and lines.

midnight grace

If you cannot find the right container for your flower design, it may be necessary to design the vase as well as the bouquet. I like this idea very much, and often use it when I cannot find a suitable vase for the arrangement I want to make. In this case, a deep rectangular vase has been wrapped with a plant called steel glass. The square that fits over the top has a circular central hole, which supports the flowers, but it can be removed and the vase used alone. Sometimes, the vase may be more striking than the flower arrangement itself: here, the flowers are used mainly as an embellishment for the container. 'Blue Curiosa' roses, which are an unusual shade of lavender, are combined with the subtle blended pinks and greens of *Astrantia major* and mauve alliums. They make a bouquet that forms a neat cluster on the top of the vase, resting on its flat surface and creating an effective contrast of shape and texture with the rigid lines of the container.

A bouquet in shades of lavender, in a container covered with steel glass, makes for a simple but very powerful design.

purple volume

Purple is the colour worn by Buddhist monks who have attained high status. This glorious arrangement, which is made with only one type of flower, the purple vanda orchid, shows how strong a colour purple is. The basic idea is to express the simple power and elegance of only a few colours. The brown of the background screen draws in another colour, which adds to the whole effect. You can use whatever flowers you like, but remember that simplicity is once again the key to success in this flower design. Ensure that you do not overcrowd the arrangement: do all you can to keep the look clean and simple, and to create an impression of volume. The principal intention of this flower arrangement is to invigorate you and uplift your spirits at the start of a new day.

This striking arrangement of purple vanda orchids, which are set inside an enclosure of green stems, is suitable for a bathroom or modern living room.

the temptations
of this world

When your soul shouts out like this, it reveals your humanity, and betrays the human weakness that is a fact of life. This boldly coloured flower design is an attempt to illustrate the trepidation of human beings who are adrift in circumstances that they do not understand. Placing the rounded vase on a tall, narrow plinth suggests the idea of human isolation. The arrangement – of red and orange arum lilies (*Zantedeschia*), red cockscombs (*Celosia*), red pincushions (*Leucospermum*), yellow and orange silkweeds (*Asclepias*) and red-hot pokers (*Kniphofia*) – illustrates the burning heat of desperate feelings. To suggest an outburst of emotion, a variety of stems, including bells-of-Ireland (*Moluccella laevis*) and guzmanias, which seem appropriately spiky, finish off the design. See how the reds and yellows seem to glow, then explode from the mass of green.

Reds, oranges and yellows emerge like glowing coals from a background of peppermint green.

Arum lily (*Zantedeschia*)

Silkweed (*Asclepias*)

Pincushion (*Leucospermum*)

Red-hot poker (*Kniphofia*)

flames of mahogany

These gorgeous mahogany sunflowers (*Helianthus*), with their glowing yellows, browns and reds, are set on an old linen *sake* bag, which is suitably dark and crumpled. The flowers and the bag complement each other perfectly. Sprigs of ivy berries have been added to provide subtle accents of colour and texture. Quite often, a successful combination of materials will suggest themselves without you having to give the choice much thought. It is at moments such as these that you will feel the power of Zen. The natural temptation is to try to control everything. Learning to listen to your inner feelings and instincts can take many years, but, once you have learned the art of listening, it will set you free. This freestyle approach to flower arranging can be both very rewarding and revealing.

Set alight these glowing mahogany colours in your room, and they will warm your heart. Let the colour and texture of the bag gather and then radiate the colours of the flowers.

a reflection
of your inner self

A bouquet can be an image of your emotions. If you wish to tell the story of your feelings in this way, think carefully about your basic colour scheme: use white, green or yellow to express emotional lightness or, for a design that is moody and dramatic, choose blue or purple. In this case, I wished to make a design that was clean, pure, simple and calm, so I chose the wonderful green of this chrysanthemum as the fundamental colour. Into this mass of greenness, I introduced white arum lilies (*Zantedeschia*) and 'Casablanca' tulips, adding small clusters of viburnum as a finishing touch. The white flowers sit well within the green chrysanthemums, and the fresh, clean design has a cheering effect on the whole room. Tulips tend to open very quickly, even in the course of an evening, so cut the stems short and arrange them tightly. Here, the stems of the tulips are slightly shorter than those of the lilies.

**Small explosions of white
and green radiate from this
beautiful cup of flowers. The
whole display is set off perfectly
by the frame of crimped
washingtonia leaves.**

flower co-ordinates

This is a contemporary design based on clean lines and simple shapes. Cylindrical vases such as this can look very effective because they have a modern look, but are also reminiscent of traditional Japanese objects. They are also useful for making bouquet designs because the form is capable of holding a considerable number of flowers. If you are going to use greens as the basis of your colour scheme, it is a good idea to use dark green as the base and highlight it with creamier shades of the same colour. This technique is much the same as the techniques of painting or photography: you are playing with light and creating contrasts. Indeed, green is a colour that needs moderating, otherwise it will overwhelm everything else. The white stones and square white base serve this purpose, as do the liberal flourishes of red, in the form of dahlias, which appear both at the top and bottom of the design. The dahlias are tempered by the addition of some chenopodiums, hollyhock buds, ivy, viburnum berries and hydrangeas.

You will need
- **square platter**
- **cylindrical vase**
- **florist's foam**
- **knife**
- **double-sided tape**
- **white stones**
- **scissors**
- **phormium leaves**
- **hydrangeas**
- **ivy**
- **viburnum berries**
- **hollyhocks (*Alcea rosea*)**
- **dahlias**
- **chenopodiums**
- **tropical fruits**

1

2

3

4

1 Stand the vase on the stone platter and fill it with well-soaked florist's foam, cut to size. Stick bands of double-sided tape around the vase and peel off the outer layer. Attach phormium leaves to the sticky surface of the tape, working from the bottom upwards.

2 Compose the bouquet, using hydrangea, ivy leaves and viburnum berries. The viburnum should constitute the central mass of the design.

3 When the florist's foam is almost covered, insert the hollyhocks to provide a colour contrast.

4 Now add the dahlias, working from the centre. Add some final accents to the design using chenopodiums and tropical fruit. Arrange a few white stones around the platter.

spirit of peonies

Flowers are living organisms and are part of the complex chain of natural life on earth. Although their forms and colours serve a practical purpose in attracting insects for pollination, they are regarded by us as objects of unparalled beauty. We nurture them in our gardens, collect and arrange them in vases, and give them to friends and family in the form of bouquets. They clearly have a far deeper significance and symbolism for us. This lovely bouquet of pink peonies (*Paeonia*) is set in front of an antique Japanese tile, so that all who look can see the heart-melting beauty of the flowers. The gentle pink tones of the flowers look perfect against this pewter-grey background. The whole display is made more poignant by the knowledge that the flowers will eventually fade away. This is irrelevant, however, when they give so much pleasure.

The pink of these outrageously beautiful peonies is given even greater prominence against a dark, antique Japanese tile.

dried loneliness

There is a moment to feel solitude as if you were

lost within a cloud. Only those who have felt

loneliness can understand the need for warmth.

DOH

FLOWER SCULPTURE

Doh means "movement", and achieving a sense of motion can contribute to the impact and success of many works of art, including sculptural flower arrangements. In trying to suggest a feeling of movement in a flower sculpture, it can be helpful to study the work of contemporary artists, such as sculptors and photographers, who often aim to create the same sense of movement in their pieces. The flower displays in this chapter are all sculptural, with clearly defined lines, and possess a powerful energy.

a sense of movement

Creating a sense of motion is possible in many different forms of art, including that of flower arranging. A stills photographer, for example, can create a very convincing simulation of movement by taking thousands of sequential shots and displaying them rapidly, one after another, in order to make a film and create an illusion of "real time" movement. This does not mean, however, that artists who create objects that are in reality static have to surrender the concept of movement to the filmmaker and confine themselves to a form that is inert and lifeless. For example, a painter can also convey an illusion of movement by creating space and light on the canvas into which the subject of the painting, whether this be a horse, a car or a dancer, can move.

Simplicity, space and light in which form can be clearly displayed: these are the basic components of the Zen room. It is in light and space that you should compose your flower sculptures if you wish to create the sense of peace and tranquillity that is essential to a relaxed atmosphere. However, calm and composure

above and right **The top of this jigsaw-like coffee table has been used as a surface for a series of stone gardens. If you can find different coloured stones, they can be used just like paint. The moss balls and gravel give additional texture to the whole design.**

should not amount to inertia, and it is possible to create a sense of harmonious tension in the arrangements that you compose and contemplate. This is achieved by the artful manipulation of natural forms and phenomena.

The geometric circle is the ideal realization of a form that exists in nature, and the human mind comprehends this instinctively; even in an object that is static, it is possible to create a sense of tension and movement by manipulating this basic form. For example, a picture taken looking up into a spiral staircase gives the impression of circles that are begun but never completed, as the line spirals towards infinity; this simple image conveys the idea of

right **Concrete can be a rather dour material. These plain concrete seats are dressed with wreaths of purple-black iris.**

below **This sculpture, which is composed of sempervivums, shows the ideal square form split in two.**

a vortex and creates a sense of danger. A circular flower design, which is divided in half, creates in the mind a sense of something as yet unattained. The two semicircles belong together and, so long as they remain apart, there is a kind of tension between them. Arrange them asymmetrically, and you can make many effective compositions, all based on the idea of an unattained ideal. The same principle applies to squares, rectangles, triangles, cones and

pyramids. Play with such shapes and fracture them in various ways until you have achieved the constructive disharmony that points to perfect harmony itself.

Certain plants lend themselves to such treament. Contorted willow, for example, makes a dramatic contrast with a long, smooth vase, as if chaotic forms are bursting out of control, and if such an arrangement is cleverly placed in light and space, you can use shadows on a wall to create even more drama. Light and the absence of light can be used exactly as if they were colours, as long as you give them sufficient space. The more cluttered a room, the less effective is the design. Because contorted willow is extremely pliable, it is possible to bend it round other objects and, because it is a linear plant, it is very good for suggesting movement, such as the flow of water or the action of a volcano: you can allow your imagination to take wing. It is wonderful for suggesting any kind of cascade or gushing phenomenon, and so is sempervivum, although the effect is slightly different. Just as some flowers bloom and become fruit, so ideas can blossom into reality. It is the same with feelings: try using sempervivum in an arrangement to suggest an outburst of emotion.

high-tech
orchids

In this design, I am showing the objects as they really are, instead of disguising functional parts and showing only a pretty front to the viewer. These phalaenopsis orchids, including the roots, are completely exposed in a transparent case. The case can be made of either glass or plastic, but remember that drilling holes in glass is much more difficult. The holes are for the creation of various "perches", using rods of steel, aluminium or plastic. The orchids can be displayed in a number of different ways. The aim of this strikingly contemporary display is to show them in all their dazzling beauty. The arrangement also has a powerful sense of movement. This is achieved as the eye of the onlooker is drawn by the curling shape of the orchid stems as they reach up and then curve downwards. There is also a strong feeling of ascent, as you climb from one rod or level to the next.

These stunning phalaenopsis, with their varying shades of pink, can be arranged on the rods in any number of ways. Create a design that you are comfortable with, and enjoy the perfection of the flowers, even for only a short time.

passion flowers and confession

When you are at one with nature, and therefore honest with yourself, it is possible to tell the truth about everything, for this is what nature demands. Nothing expresses this emotional nakedness so clearly as the passion flower when its petals are wide open and its very heart is exposed. Such poignant vulnerability deserves respect, and in giving respect to nature all the materials should be appropriate. This pottery vase is made from clay and its base is surrounded with pebbles that are millions of years old. Different types of passion flower (*Passiflora*) in and around the vase express the idea of emerging emotions. The stems of these flowers are curved, like gentle feelings, and if you cut them long enough to make crossovers, there is no better way to create a visual embrace. Tiny pink silkweeds (*Asclepias*) add a finishing touch.

Gentle emotions are curved, like the waves of the sea and the stems of these exquisite passion flowers, which are locked in a sweet embrace.

flower composition

Because flowers are never quite the same, and because the canvas of the imagination is unlimited, there is endless scope when planning a floral composition. If you notice the geometry of nature, it will speak to you and give you guidance. This composition illustrates the richness of natural geometry and is designed to hang on a wall.

The components can be arranged in a number of different ways, thus giving the design a sense of implied movement. Orange and yellow roses and carnations (*Dianthus*) are combined with tulips, green sedums and bells-of-Ireland (*Moluccella laevis*) to form a mass of fresh colours and to fill you with the optimism of spring.

The closer you look at this mass of colours, lines and forms, the more you will be amazed.

Rosa 'Milva'

Dianthus 'Prada'

Rosa 'Startrix'

Tropical fruits and sedums

the heart of a flower

If you look into the heart of a flower and allow what you find there to affect your inner feelings, those feelings will begin to multiply and soon your mind will be full of bright ideas. Flowers give you strength and inspiration. Arum lilies (*Zantedeschia*) make a dramatic gesture in this modernist room where the surfaces are plain and the colours light. The flowing forms and the graduating yellows and purples of the arum lilies look wonderful when set in a dark green cup of livistona leaves, the radiating lines of which are so clean and strong. To complete this powerful combination and counter the straight lines in the design, and in the room, the curving leaves of phormium have been allowed to spray outwards like tentacles, or hang loosely in flowing lines. Arum lilies last about a week, but it is not wise to use the leaves with the flowers for, once cut, they are too weak to take up water, and wither very quickly.

The flowing lines of **Phormium tenax** give rhythm to this design, while its simple setting gives it dramatic power.

Arum lily (*Zantedeschia*)

Phormium leaves and arum lilies

silver zone

Each of the sculptural forms in this design is part of a pair, the idea being that the relationship, the tension and movement between them, enhances their purity. As it is with flowers, so it is with people: their full potential is never realized in isolation.

Many people think that the creation of flower sculptures is difficult, but it is both difficult and simple, like everything in life, art and Zen: once you have gained a little confidence in yourself and what you are doing, it can be great fun and you can enjoy yourself. This design uses the idea of positive and negative shapes to suggest the relationship between masculine and feminine, as it is conceived in the yin and yang of Chinese philosophy. Two interlockable kidney shapes cut from florist's foam symbolize man and woman. These are covered with the silver leaves of *Leucadendron argenteum*, then finished off with purple tracheliums. Remember to vary the design of each shape, for "the difference" is most important, as everyone knows, and one sculptured flower must charm the other.

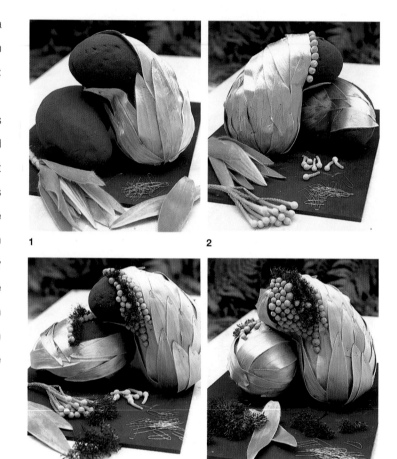

1

2

3

4

You will need
- florist's foam
- knife
- florist's wire
- wire cutters
- scissors
- *Leucadendron argenteum* leaves
- *Brunia albiflora*
- tracheliums

1 Carve a pair of complementary shapes from the well-soaked florist's foam. Cut a number of short strands of florist's wire and bend them into hairpin shapes to attach the leaves. Take one of the forms and, beginning at the bottom, use the hairpin wires to cover the foam shapes with the silver leaves of *Leucadendron argenteum*.

2 When both forms are almost completely covered, lay them together beside the remaining silver leaves. The shapes, and the relationship between them, are entirely up to you. Embellish the basic forms with whatever patterns you choose. Start with clusters of *Brunia albiflora*.

3 Continue adding the clusters of *Brunia albiflora* over the base of silver leaves, and add purple tracheliums as an accent.

4 When you have decorated your forms and decided how to "marry" them together, use any remaining leaves or shoots to embellish the heads and finalize the design.

cool energy

This display of lilies and slipper orchids (*Paphiopedilum*), which would look striking in a bathroom or on a table in the dining room, is immersed in water in a cylindrical vase of clear glass. Nothing could be simpler. The composition is more complex than this, however, as it displays at least three of the elements that are essential to life itself: air, water and light. A sense of movement is created as the water, light and air all swirl around the bowl. As light shines through the glass, it reveals a mass of flower petals in an explosion of colour: gorgeous pinks and reds, yellows, greens and whites. This mass seems to pulse with its own energy, sending out waves of beauty and goodness.

From the cool environs of a water-filled glass, this mass of orchids and lilies vibrates with life-giving energy.

fading into time

It's not how much time you have spent,

but how beautifully you have spent that time.

SEI

STILL-LIFE
FLORAL ART

Stillness is the subject of this chapter. That which possesses *sei,* or stillness, is beautiful and refreshing, clear and unreserved, but even that which is pure will fade away, as all things fade away: flowers and trees, rocks and mountains, until the process, whatever it is, comes to its unknown conclusion. The sense of contingency, an awareness that all things are ephemeral, is highly developed in Zen, and it is the contingency of things, large or small, that gives them poignancy, so that an exploding star, or a flower that will die by the end of the day, are equally moving.

creating a work of art

Sensitivity to the impermanence of the natural world makes us receptive to the vibrancy of single, living things, and when we create something we feel its minute reverberations in time, the ripples of its existence. Cut flowers are beautiful, tender and temporary. When they are painted, however, their fleeting existence is granted indefinite duration, and a painting of flowers, if skilfully executed, can lead back to the moment when they flourished. Let us try to make arrangements that have the charm of the works of the old masters. Their paintings express feelings that came from their souls.

When attempting to reproduce a still-life painting in a flower arrangement, it is necessary to consider its composition carefully. Observe the texture and colour of the background as precisely as you observe the colours and textures of all the objects in the picture. The balance of forms, colours and textures is never accidental. No matter how natural and spontaneous the overall effect may be, the artist has given serious consideration to everything. However, you

must never allow your knowledge of this fact to inhibit your own creativity, for the secret of flower arranging is to follow the flowers. Allow your sensibilities to be guided by them. As with all forms of art, the mere exposition of technique is never enough; it is not sufficient to learn the laws of composition and implement them like a robot, for then the whole purpose is lost. The final point of flower arranging is the free expression of your feelings, and the best way to find this freedom is to know exactly what you are doing, so that it becomes second nature. Think first, study the painting until you have absorbed the artist's feeling for form, texture and colour, then free yourself from his or her influence and do as you wish, simply and instinctively.

If you wish to make flower arrangements in Zen style, it is a good idea to study the mandala, the Buddhist representation of the universe, and its Japanese form, the *mandara*, noting the special feeling for form

above right **The purple-brown of these bananas makes a perfect match with the orchids against a dark screen.**

left **Red-hot pokers (*Kniphofia*) and deep purple campanulas are the only constituents of this simple design.**

and the rich variety of textures and colours used in traditional Japanese art. Base your themes on seasons of the year, periods of history, ancient or modern styles. For example, if you decide to make autumn the basic theme of your design, you should first carefully consider what autumn means to you. For me, this season suggests a time of deep contemplation, a time to reflect upon earthly existence – as plants and flowers change form and colour and eventually pass from this life, they remind us of our own mortality.

For a still-life flower design that is contemporary but also reflects the Zen tradition, it is a good idea to use a container that is simple, but shapely in form and monochrome in colour. This will give your arrangement a modern look. It is also advisable to use a limited number of flowers, to consider each bloom and to think carefully about the combination of form and colour. A simple but beautiful design can be made with a single line of flowers placed against a plain background. Here, the skill lies in using utter simplicity, but avoiding

above right and left
Here, a single leaf has been set on a small, white bowl and placed next to a plain, black bowl, containing the light brown carnation, *Dianthus* 'Terra Nova'. The resulting still-life is perfect.

coldness or hardness in the final result. It is helpful to plan out your design first. Make a dotted line along a sheet of paper, then draw or paint your arrangement using this line as a guide, and consider the mass and form of each flower as it relates to the rest of the design. Soon, the forms, textures and colours of the flowers and other objects will begin to "speak" to you. Not only the flowers, but such everyday objects as glasses, flowerpots and candleholders will acquire the status of beautiful objects when given the care and respect that all things deserve; soon, you will be listening to the language of objects, and your simple design will have become something beautiful.

Even in a world that is full of pollution and impurity, it is possible to rediscover the purity of simple things; all you have to do is stand still for a moment, and look, really look. By such uncomplicated means you may find the elixir that relieves the aridity of daily existence.

the captive
moment

When you have lost your way, try standing still for a moment, hold your breath, and watch yourself as if you were an outside observer: you will see yourself as you really are. Just as it is possible to capture such glimpses of yourself and regain your sense of perspective, so it is possible to glimpse the reality of other entities, and this is what I try to do with my flower designs. I love combinations of flowers and fruit, and here I have made a pyramid of them, set them in a black basket and placed them on a very solid and imposing antique sideboard, so that they tumble like a carefree, feminine flourish on top of something rather masculine. They go well together. Unless you are intent on making your design deliberately modern, in which case you should use a pastel or monochrome colour scheme, remember that combinations of flowers and fruit look wonderful in time-worn settings full of dark hues, which show off the richness of natural colours.

Luscious fruits, such as plums and currants, are combined with globe artichoke buds, pink roses, poppy seedheads, sempervivums and a single pitcher plant (*Sarracenia*), as well as some elegant vine and pelargonium leaves.

autumn calm

Autumn suggests a time to reflect upon earthly existence; as plants and flowers change form and colour, they remind us of our mortality. It is a melancholy but beautiful season. Surround yourself with the soft, warm colours appropriate to this time of year and, as you arrange your flowers in recognition of all that fades away, give silent thanks that soon there will be another spring to enjoy. A few touches of cold colour will acknowledge the intervening winter. For this arrangement, a dark brass bowl is dressed with white hydrangeas to provide an accent, but pomegranates are the main feature, for these fruits, so rich and full of goodness, symbolize the season of fruitfulness. Their skin displays perfectly the transition from green through yellow to reddish brown, as living things turn from the sun to face the bleakness of winter. Marking a farewell to summer, sweet peas (*Lathyrus odoratus*) make a delicate finishing touch in contrast with the heavier forms of the pomegranates.

This mellow arrangement beside a lovely silk-covered armchair makes a perfect invitation to settle down for a rest.

heartstrings

When the winter is over and the warm weather returns, the new season's flowers begin to play on our heartstrings, and even if the music that you hear is not what you used to hear, you will learn to enjoy it. Each new day should be celebrated, so why not do so with an arrangement of spring and summer flowers? This arrangement may appear easy, for there is an abundance of flowers to choose from, but they should not be thrown together haphazardly. Poppies (*Papaver*) form the back and front of this design, with globe artichokes (*Cynara scolymus*) between them. Once the basic shape is established, other

Poppy (*Papaver*)

Globe artichoke (*Cynara scolymus*)

Globe artichoke bud

Astrantia major

varieties can be added. Poppies give you highlights, whereas globe artichokes are subtle in their colouring and pale pink *Astrantia major* is subtler still. Once you have started to achieve sufficient density, concentrate on variety, filling the gaps with scabious (*Scabiosa*), lotus seedheads, hydrangeas and blue-berried viburnum. Be conscious at all times of the colour combinations, for it is easy to go over the top, and moderate the brightest colours with plenty of green foliage.

above **Spring and summer flowers will pluck your heartstrings and play the music that you wish to hear.**

black temptation

Flowers, like all living things, can create excitement and passion, but floral art can also help you to understand the contingency of earthly existence. This richly coloured arrangement is an attempt to capture the true nature of everyday things that we usually take for granted. Indeed, fruit is usually regarded as a commodity that is stacked on supermarket shelves, bought and eaten, then used or discarded. However, if you look closely at the sensual forms of these beautiful black grapes and ripe plums or the burgeoning seedlets of the ripening blackberries, you will start to understand both the beauty and the transitoriness of existence. Of all the flowers that can arouse such feelings, there is perhaps nothing to compare with the intense, velvety blooms of *Cosmos atrosanguineus,* the chocolate cosmos, which are included in the design.

Chocolate cosmos (*Cosmos atrosanguineus*)

These beautiful blooms of chocolate cosmos have been arranged very naturally; they really speak for themselves.

Plums, grapes and blackberries

finite existence

Nothing lasts forever. Everything on earth will eventually fade away. When you create your flower designs you should bear in mind the emphemeral nature and contingency of all living things, especially flowers. Flower compositions will, of course, last for just a short time, once the flowers have been cut, so try to plan your designs very carefully before you begin to construct them. In the case of this free design, you will need to assemble all the basic elements first, including the square stone tablet, the stone vase and the little black pot; then consider all the placements and the angles of the flowers until you are quite clear about your objectives. When you see how lovely the purple gloxinia will look on the stone tablet or peeping from the head of the vase, then, and only then, will you be ready to use them.

You will need
- cream board
- black pebbles
- square stone tablet
- stone vase
- black pot
- scissors
- 2 avocados
- 2 sanseveria leaves
- 3 pots gloxinia
- woody bear
- sedum

1 **Put the cream board in place and surround it with black pebbles. Place the stone tablet slightly off-centre and position the stone vase next to it.**

2 **Consider the composition carefully and place the avocados in what you feel to be their best position.**

3 **Arrange the sanseveria leaves in the stone vase. Consider the balance between the cluster of gloxinia blooms on the tablet and those reserved for the vase. Adjust the avocados accordingly.**

4 **Take a gloxinia plant from its pot, clean the roots and place it in the vase with the two sanseveria leaves. Consider the composition again and add more blooms of gloxinia wherever necessary. Finish off with woody bear and sedum, and place the small black pot on the board.**

1

2

3

4

stillness

The inspiration for this design comes from the old masters, who knew exactly how to capture a moment in time. In a setting that is deliberately antique, the palette is a strong one, using the flowers as paint. Vivid red cockscombs (*Celosia*), white pumpkins, reddish-pink peaches and other fruits, including blueberries, raspberries and a pineapple, are set against a rustic background. The aim is to bring to life what is, in a conventional design, a natural blind-spot. So, the frame is tilted to focus on the bottom right-hand corner. The display is arranged in this corner, the point being that if the frame were set at the usual angle and the design set in the centre-ground, as normal, then the viewer's eye would not be drawn to the bottom right-hand corner. We can all find places of our own in which to flourish; it is not necessary to be centre-stage.

The strong colours of this design bring to life the corner of the picture frame.

nostalgic
blue

People try to beautify their memory

and to transform it into a treasure of

the heart. Why?

MANDALA
FLOWER
CONSTRUCTION

The Buddhist mandala is a cosmic map, a diagram of sacred territory, the precinct in which enlightenment takes place. *Manda* means essence, and *la* means attainment, so the mandala is a representation of the state of enlightenment. Mandalas are not simply works of art, but works of religious art – sacred artefacts, the dwelling places of gods. The flower designs in this chapter are based on shapes, such as squares and circles, which are iconic forms in the mandalas of Esoteric Buddhism.

the importance of form

At some time around the year 450BC, Siddhartha Gautama – the Shakyamuni Buddha – sat beneath a tree and meditated for 49 days and nights, having vowed that he would "not get up from this place" until he had found the "truth" from the inside rather than the outside. It was there that he experienced enlightenment, and devotees regard the place where he sat, known as the *bodhimanda,* as sacred. To this day, Tibetan monks mark out a circle on the ground with coloured sand and construct a symbolic diagram before performing their holy rites. Afterwards, they sweep away the sand to erase the diagram and leave the place undefiled. The disc, a circular diagram with a sacred centre, is a kind of mandala.

A mandala may have three dimensions, the sacred spot being marked by a statue or holy object, but the kind found in most shrines and temples take the form of paintings. These contain images of gods in human form, or symbolic forms or even Sanskrit letters that represent sacred figures. Although such mandalas are two-dimensional, they are meant to be changed by the imagination into three-dimensional images of sacred places. The devotee begins with a kind of map that he or she must transform in the course of contemplation.

The practice of using mandalas as aids to meditation is typical of the Esoteric Buddhism that reached Japan in the 6th century and remained dominant until the 9th century. The esoteric mandalas that feature either circles or squares, and radiate outwards from a sacred centre, were introduced to Japan by Kukai, a Japanese monk who had studied under the Chinese master, Huiguo, in Chang'an, then the capital of China, in 805AD. Kukai's discipleship, and this exchange of knowledge, is a perfect example of religious and cultural cross-fertilization, known as syncretism. Kukai made popular an entirely distinctive form of sacred art in Japan, where the pan-Asian mandala was transformed into the *mandara*, which is distinctly Japanese in both inspiration and style.

All mandalas, whether pan-Asian or distinctly Japanese, have the primary purpose of providing devotees with the stimulation and the means to undertake a spiritual journey. The idea is that pilgrims should remove themselves physically and mentally from the circumstances of their everyday lives. In the case of esoteric mandalas, pilgrims pass through portals or over bridges, which are often guarded by demonic masks whose purpose is to repel evil spirits.

left **This truncated cone of dark purple-red roses sits perfectly on a cube dressed with camellia leaves. This is an abstract version of the Buddhist mandala.**

right above **Any fruit with a silvery sheen creates a striking effect on a small silver dish.**

right below **Figs have a sensuous quality that is hard to define. In this design, the effect has been multiplied by placing groups of figs on a mirror.**

They traverse the outer courts and halls before entering the cosmic realms, where they communicate with the god or gods at the heart of both the mandala and the universe. It is here that the devotees seek and find understanding of the great truths.

One of the impulses that led to the establishment of Esoteric Buddhism was a protest at the impossibility, according to orthodox texts, of attaining enlightenment in the course of a human lifetime. Esoterics believed in the three mysteries of body, speech and mind, and held that enlightenment could be approached through sensory experiences: through bodily rituals known as *mudras*, verbal rituals known as *mantras* and mental rituals involving mandalas. When the pilgrim penetrates to the heart of the mandala and unites himself or herself with the ultimate Buddha nature, the barriers between this world and the sacred world are removed, thus enabling the Zen follower to reach enlightenment.

My designs constitute a small act of homage, a nod in the direction of Kukai. They echo the square and circular motifs to be found in the mandala, and they offer to you, I hope, the opportunity to create within your own home a small oasis of tranquillity, something that will bring you closer to the world of *satori,* or enlightenment.

silky orange

The islands of Japan lie at the end of the Silk Road, the great ancient trading route which carried not only goods but ideas to and from the civilizations of Asia. Nowadays, Nepal, some parts of Tibet and Japan are the only countries in which the mandala remains popular. To symbolize the Silk Road and tell the story of the mandala's arrival in Japan, five silver pots stand in a straight line. In keeping with the monochrome regularity of the pots, only a single kind of flower has been used. The petals of the silkweed (*Asclepias*) are tiny and delicate, so with great care I have made a little bouquet for each pot. I chose the bathroom for this arrangement because it is an ideal place to relax, and to contemplate the ancient history of Asia. Just thinking about the millions of merchants who plied the great Silk Road over thousands of years makes one dizzy: where are they now? Such thoughts moderate any sense of self-importance and put the ego in its place.

Test your abilities by making a simple bouquet from one kind of flower, in this case silkweeds, and playing with the various tones of a single colour to achieve variety.

paradox

This display is based on a koan, which is a philosophical topic, word or phrase that cannot be solved intellectually and is given to the Zen student to help his or her journey beyond his conceptual mind to the realm beyond thought. For example, there is no logical answer to the question, "What is the sound of one hand clapping?" This is because the question is paradoxical. However, it is still stimulating: what is this hearing and seeing, this clapping and moving that exist only in the mind? Such a question prompts you to consider these concepts afresh, and you start thinking about the limitless freedom of the human imagination. This design symbolizes the birth of a paradoxical idea by showing the light as it emerges from a flower. From a purely aesthetic point of view, the purple blooms of morning glory (*Ipomoea*) look beautiful combined with green and silver. If you shine a light through the whole arrangement, the effect is simply magical.

The light shining through this display represents the birth of a paradoxical idea.

the map of the mandala

The mandala is a cosmic map, a diagram of sacred territory, the precinct in which enlightenment takes place. In order to symbolize this Buddhist icon, this arrangement is based on the large, circular form of the sunflower (*Helianthus*) and to emphasize the dark brown disc at the heart of each flower, I stripped off the yellow petals, leaving only the green calyx. Having established the circular form of the sunflower as the basic motif, it was then countered with linear plants – bamboo canes and the stems of *Cyperus alternifolius* – to make a strong, simple

Sunflower (*Helianthus*)   **Amaranthus caudatus**

Bamboo and *Cyperus alternifolius*   **Zingiber zerumbet**

design. The bamboo is very effective, but, because it makes such a powerful counterpoint, it was necessary to modify the contrast. Adding a few blooms of red love-lies-bleeding (*Amaranthus caudatus*), orange eucalyptus berries and lime-green *Zingiber zerumbet* gave the design the accent it needed and linked the principal motifs. In the final result, circular shapes predominate, but they are not too overpowering.

The circular brown heart of the sunflower, stripped of its yellow petals, makes a perfect match with the brown background.

the mandala's composition

Although each mandala illustrates a different characteristic of the Buddha, and all mandalas are therefore slightly different, they are drawn in accordance with clearly defined rules and are arranged systematically. For this flower design depicting the mandala, a lovely black, slightly bellied vase sets the basic form. The plants have been chosen for their tightly packed, wavy lines, setting off the deep red blooms of pelargoniums with the dark green of wandflower (*Galax*), and linking the main colours with the light red of a few stems of translucent redcurrants. The effect sought, in this combination of a potent-looking container and a tightly bunched display of flowers, is one of power and emerging energy, for the mandala is in no sense inert; it is made for a purpose and meant to be used.

Variety of form and texture can be found in just a few different plants. The black vase goes well with a glass-topped table and a black leather chair. Simplicity of line and form is essential to minimalism.

mellow crimson

The subtle gradation of colouring in these grapes suggests feelings of mellowness. Ripened fruit, with its association with autumn, is often used to suggest reflective feelings and even slight melancholy. Because grapes are also globular, they are very useful for representing the mandala. They have been used here in combination with the green seedheads of poppies (*Papaver*) in order to emphasize the circular motif found in all esoteric mandalas. In this way, several related concepts have been married. Feelings of mellowness and melancholy are associated not only with the fruits of autumn, but also with religious sentiments, and it is for the exercise and expression of such emotions that the mandala was first conceived. The rectangular platform on which the design has been placed again makes reference to the mandala, the rectangle being another iconic form to be found in all esoteric mandalas.

These two bouquets, both rich and full of life, are attracted to each other by their differences.

balancing opposites

Esoteric mandalas – or *mandaras*, as they became in Japan – consist of circles, usually circles within squares. To create a flower design in mandala mood, you should use the circle as the basic motif. This display uses the dark brown heart of the sunflower (*Helianthus*) as its fundamental shape. A square table forms the base and on it is set a spherical vase of exactly the right size, thus fulfilling the first requirement of any floral design, which is to match the right materials and forms. When choosing the vase, take into account the colours of the flowers. Note that the flowers in this design contain both bright and dark colours, so ensure that the colour of the vase is moderated precisely by the flowers. Red is a symbol of the human life force, but it should be used with purpose, not indiscriminately.

You will need
- spherical vase
- string
- scissors
- philodendron leaf
- brown sunflowers (*Helianthus*)
- red robin (*Cotinus*)
- love-lies-bleeding (*Amaranthus caudatus*)
- eucalyptus berries

1   2   3   4

1 Fill the vase with water and position it centrally on the square table. Arrange a philodendron leaf on the left-hand side.

2 Carefully balance the lengths of the brown sunflowers. Bind the stems together, concealing the binding under the flowerheads, and place the bunch in the vase. Check that the height of the design does not overbalance the vase.

3 Add sunflowers to the original structure until you have just the right number, then add some stems of red robin. Check the balance of the colours.

4 Dress the base of the vase with a few stems of *Amaranthus caudatus*, eucalyptus berries and red robin to balance the arrangement, until you are satisfied that the design is finished.

an abstraction

Kukai was the Buddhist monk who introduced the mandala to Japan at the beginning of the 9th century, so it is fair to say that he was the first Japanese to be charmed by its beauty. Apart from the religious significance of the mandala, it may have been the logical coherence and abstract perfection of the form that unlocked his heart. Using a low, round vase and a transparent, six-sided table, the design alludes strongly to this abstract perfection. Simplicity is vital, but coldness is anathema, so to counter the whiteness and lightness of everything else, this bouquet is made of richly coloured cockscombs (*Celosia*). These flowers, so abundant in texture, come in a wide variety of colours, and this kind of composition, although apparently simple, allows considerable scope for tonal invention. However many you make, each one will be different, and because the basic form is so strong, each one will look lovely.

The densely ruffled flowers of cockscombs create a perfect, contemporary-looking display in a vase on a transparent, hexagonal table.

eternal love

Universal love, which lasts eternally,

only exists in hearts that are free.

BASSARA
ZEN ART

It might be said that artistic activity is itself a
manifestation of nature; there is no real division
between the creative force of the universe and
the human desire to make beautiful things.
There is no limitation to what may be created.
The artistic mind is free; the artist is at liberty to
make existence from non-existence, to create
something *bassara* – new or novel – from
nothing, prompted only by intuition and flashes
of inspiration.

floral inspiration

Inspiration comes when the mind is emptied and contact is made with the inner self, the universe within; there is no limit to the ways in which our internal resources may be tapped. Today, the Zen monk is highly disciplined and has many aids to concentration developed over the centuries, but in the early days of the Zen masters, training methods were not defined, and each individual was obliged to plumb the depths of his own spiritual darkness in the search for enlightenment. In the same way, we must find our own paths through the dark forest of human experience; then, if we try hard enough – and we are lucky – we will find the sunlit glades in which good and beautiful things can be made.

Bassara means "novelty", but the desire to create novelty should be regarded with circumspection. To me, wholeness, harmony and radiance are and always will be the necessary requirements of

beauty, and when I seek novelty, I do so by emptying my mind and opening myself to things as they are, for the riches of nature are inexhaustible, and there is always something new to be found. Novelty is under our noses: in our everyday lives, right here in our own homes and gardens, and in order to find it, all we have to do is look afresh at what has already been given to us; that is to say, light and space, darkness and light, colour, texture, sound and smell – everything that exists in the palette of nature.

When giving rein to your powers of expression, for example, it is not necessary to be literal-minded: a vase does not have to be a vase. It is possible to take thin sheets of stainless steel, or any other suitable material, and make them into shapes that suggest the idea of a vase. Stainless steel is very useful for this kind of metaphorical design because it is a monochrome material and

can easily be curled or bent and formed into rectangular, triangular, cylindrical or conical vase-like shapes. This material is a favourite of mine, especially in combination with arum lilies (*Zantedeschia*), because the coldness and brilliance of the steel contrasts so well with the beautiful, tender petals and slender green stems of the flowers.

Cold brilliance provides a sense of distance in a design, a quality known in Japanese culture as *ma*. However, the supply of materials for making or suggesting containers is virtually unlimited, and there are also thousands of flowers from which to choose; when you wish to create an original and striking design, all you need is imagination. You, too, can make flower arrangements just as you please, but by responding with sensitivity to the shapes, colours and textures of your materials, you will avoid the incongruous. It is possible to achieve novelty without descending into the absurd or

above far left **This sheaf of red rice has been tied near the top in order to avoid cutting the long, elegant stems.**

below far left **In this novel design, a column of bananas has been placed in a simple, cup-like, black bowl. Bird-of-paradise (*Strelitzia*) provides the necessary accent.**

left and below left **A bird-of-paradise (*Strelitzia*) against a dark background suggests the emergence of new-found hope.**

ridiculous. The floral arrangements shown in this chapter aim to create novel and unusual effects by combining and contrasting unlikely shapes and textures.

The two sheaf-like arrangements shown here are particularly unusual because the visual emphasis has been switched from the heads of the plants, which are normally the centre of attention in a flower design, to the beautiful, straight, strong stems. In the wider arrangement on the opposite page, the delicate heads of red rice were spread out, as were the stems at the bottom of the design, until a balance of emphasis was achieved. However, in the tall arrangement, above, I was looking for a clear change from the norm. Both these arrangements suggest a sense of disciplined constraint, masking power and potential, but you will, of course, interpret them in your own way.

image-making

Look around until you find something that suggests a vase; if the object goes well with your flowers, all you need now is imagination. The basis of this design is a dried banana leaf, set on top of an antique chest. Because the lines of *Heliconia* 'Sexy Pink' and the foxtail lilies (*Eremurus*) are vertical, the horizontal line of the banana leaf provides balance. Heliconia is a hanging plant, with striking tones of pink and green, and it is very good for making a tropical display. In order to give the design the necessary volume, several stems of yellow eremurus stand alongside the heliconia, and the whole arrangement is finished with a cluster of anthurium leaves. Heliconia is a tropical plant, and should be maintained at a temperature above 15°C (59°F).

Heliconia 'Sexy Pink' and yellow foxtail lilies (Eremurus) look great together and create a tidy arrangement with parallel lines. The spiky aechmea at the front of the design has an explosive effect.

the power of
emerald green

It is a good idea, before you begin making your design, to conceive and compose its theme, for then, with a clear picture in mind, you will find your work that much easier. This design is an attempt to make a bouquet which is based on a green colour theme. The white peonies (*Paeonia*) provide an accent to enhance the principal tone. The bouquet sits on two horizontally aligned bamboo shoots, which give strength of line and variety of texture to the design. Green hydrangea flowerheads with pink-tinged petals are also included. However, the composition is not complete until the addition of two huge, dipping leaves of *Curculigo capitulata,* which finish it with a magnificent flourish. The leaves of *Curculigo capitulata* are not only just the right colour, but their size, shape and texture provide the perfect modulating inflection to the tightly clustered flowers at the centre of the design.

With colour as the central motif, the starting point for this design was a bunch of *Rosa* 'Emerald Green', set in a bouquet with green anthuriums, kangaroo paws, hydrangeas, and snake grass (*Scirpus tabernaemontani*).

thinking power

A seed germinates, a plant grows, a flower blooms and the whole process comes to fruition. Or, to use another metaphor, a tiny trickle of ideas can develop into a flood, even a mighty river; small ideas are important, and we should try to nurture them. Here, a solid, ivory-coloured stone vase, which curves beautifully from base to rim, is filled with the cockscomb, *Celosia argentea cristata*. The tightly packed petals of this plant suggest the shape and texture of the human brain. From this mysterious organ, seething with electrical and chemical activity, great ideas come and powerful emotions explode like solar eruptions. As an emblem of such explosions, nothing seemed more suitable than a giant heliconia, planted in the centre of the skull-vase and the brain-plants. Whether or not you accept the metaphor, this huge plant is a most magnificent specimen. I hope that the cool shape and colour of the vase counterbalance such an extravagant gesture.

This kind of vase, so simple and so solid, is very good for sizeable arrangements, and very typical of Zen.

flower boat

This simple but effective design uses objects that happened to be handy. A long, slightly curved banana leaf was ideal for the purpose of suggesting the idea of a boat – it is reminiscent of a Venetian gondola. You may or may not possess a dried banana leaf, but you can of course use any large leaf of similar shape to form the basis of your design. A gently curling leaf of *Curculigo capitulata* has been placed on top of the dried banana leaf to reinforce the horizontal line of the design. In order to give the shape maximum impact, a vertical branch of contorted willow rises from the centre, dressed with beautiful, brown-spotted Cambria orchids. These flowers demand close inspection if their fragile, delicate glory is to be fully revealed and

Cambria orchid   ***Kalanchoë thyrsiflora*** **and anthuriums**

appreciated. At the base of the vertical "mast", red anthuriums and *Kalanchoë thyrsiflora* leaves complete the design. These are quite different in shape, colouring and texture from the delicate Cambria orchids. Using a few simple things, it is possible to compose a wonderful variety of textures, shapes and colours: this is the point at which the design should be left alone. It is clear that this design echoes the classical Japanese styles of *rikka* (erect) and *seika* (living plant) flower arrangements. The basic form of the design, with a vertical element in the exact centre of the platform, is typical of this style.

Vertical contorted willow and a horizontal banana leaf give this arrangement a strong visual presence. An elegant, green *Curculigo capitulata* leaf brings a contrast of colour to the brown banana leaf.

the ashes of happiness

We must know the depths of sorrow before we can experience true happiness. This is a truth known only to adults, and I have therefore expressed it in a suitable style, using red, black and silver in a design made for a city living room. Although, like the colours, the idea may be sophisticated, the actual construction is simple, as befits a Zen composition. The ashes of sorrow are represented by sticks of silvery black charcoal, bundled together with silver florist's wire and set in a square black tray on a small rectangular table. The wire has an aesthetic purpose as well as a practical one, for its silver colouring accents the sheen of the blackened charcoal. In the midst of this pyre, cuttings of gladioli emerge like hope, and beautiful blood-red roses may be taken for the blooming of new-found passion. Of course, you will make your own interpretation of this and every other design, but this theme seems well expressed by red and black, and if you wish to develop it in Zen style, cylindrical and rectangular shapes are useful. The sticks of charcoal are also very practical in an urban environment, for they cleanse the air that you breathe.

1

2

3

4

You will need
- charcoal
- string
- 2 square black trays
- rectangular table
- silver florist's wire
- florist's foam
- scissors
- *Gladiolus* 'Sweet Shadow'
- *Rosa* 'Black Baccara'

1 Tightly tie the first seven sticks of charcoal with string or florist's wire. Place the charcoal in the centre of a square tray set inside a larger tray, and place the arrangement on the table.

2 Surround the central column with shorter sticks of charcoal and tie the whole thing with silver florist's wire, filling the crevices between the sticks with soaked florist's foam as you go to form a base for the flowers.

3 Starting at the bottom, introduce stems of gladioli to the design, being careful not to use too many, for simplicity is the soul of Zen. It is also important to see that the petals are small, so that they do not diminish the impact of the roses.

4 Finish the design with the dark red roses, using them to enhance the sculptural quality of the charcoal and create maximum impact.

light and shadow

Light and shadow appear to be independent, but they exist side by side eternally, for shadow is merely the absence of light. The colours of this design create a sense of opposition. When white anthuriums are set against a dark background, their whiteness becomes more vivid and the contrast is stark. The flowers are beautiful seen in close-up, but they also look splendid in a cluster at the foot of a soaring background. Anthuriums, which originate in the West Indies and the Torrid Zone of the Americas, come in a variety of shapes and colours, so there is scope for invention when you are looking for a dramatic contrast that will show the flowers to best effect. They are usually widely available throughout the year, and they are durable flowers if they are kept in the right conditions. Because they are tropical, they do not like the cold, but if you provide them with a temperature of at least 15°C (59°F), they should last for two to three weeks.

The pure whiteness of these anthurium flowers seems to glow against the rich chocolate-brown of the screen.

a seduction of
pomegranates

Desire is only a shade of your mind at the time.

SATORI
FLOWERS FOR MEDITATION

Satori is enlightenment, and the attainment of enlightenment is the ultimate objective of all those who practise *zazen*, or the art of meditation. The search for enlightenment is a journey of rediscovery. The Zen practitioner searches within for his or her own true nature, and the search is a perpetual one. The arrangements in this chapter are designed to help you relax, meditate and make contact with yourself in a calm, tranquil atmosphere.

finding enlightenment

We meditate to free ourselves from the desires that seem so necessary for survival, but which cause us so much misery; with a calm and quiet mind, we seek freedom from anxiety. As with anything else, language can delude us, and if we think of "practice", "pursuit", "striving" and "attainment" in the usual way, we may deceive ourselves by thinking that enlightenment is just like the other things we seek: if we are honest, work hard and do the right things, we can acquire what we want. But if we seek to grasp this "thing" from the world, we delude ourselves. *Nirvana* is not some fantastic condition in which all worldly desires are satisfied. It is a state of mind, the realization that everything is one, both oneness and nothingness; that distinctions between good and bad, sacred and profane, *samsara* (rebirth) and *nirvana* (final release), the Buddha and oneself, are worldly delusions. This realization is *kensho*, the first step on the path to enlightenment. It is a most important step, opening the mind and the heart to a new experience of reality.

left **The stretched pyramidal shape of these copper vases enhances the striking design. They are an ideal setting for stems of zazen grass.**

below left **Water lilies, set on a giant leaf of *Curculigo capitulata*, float calmly in a brown bowl, the colour of which tones with the purple-red flowers.**

A Zen master, asked what is attained from enlightenment, is likely to say nothing, or that there is nothing to attain. The questioner is thinking in the wrong way, as an individual who seeks something from the world, and it is not until he or she realizes that there is nothing for which to strive – because everything is already present in him or herself – that anything has been "attained" at all. The search for peace of mind in an environment that militates relentlessly against it is difficult, but it is like all things in Zen: both difficult and simple. You may take the path of the disciple and accept the discipline of *zazen*, dedicating your life to a search for the Buddha nature within you, but even Buddhist monks have to live. They have to work, clean and wash up; they know the importance of searching for peace in everyday life.

left **These
wonderful, elegant
stems of snake
grass (*Scirpus
tabernaemontani*)
set in a bed of
blue-black pebbles
provide the perfect
aid to meditation in
a Japanese house.**

We, too, can learn to relax by allowing ourselves time to meditate, and even if this has to be relatively short it is still possible to make little oases of peace and quiet. Make yourself a small Zen garden in which the moss and plants, the stones, sand and water are all treated with tenderness and respect. Sit and gaze at a beautiful flower until your own nature and that of the flower are one, your heart is peaceful and your mind is quiet. Then, when you have emptied your mind and released yourself from anxiety, your innermost feelings will come to the surface. Fresh ideas will present themselves, as if by magic, but there is, of course, nothing magical about it; you have simply allowed yourself to be free for a moment, and it is in such moments that you conceive new designs that express your true feelings.

transcending
chance

The lotus flower is a fundamental motif in Buddhist religious imagery, and is used in many ways. A central branch on a platform represents the Buddha, and this structure is known as *rikka:* an arrangement that is standing or erect. Here is the lotus flower (*Nelumbo*) in all its glory. The platform is a large, shallow dish, heaped with black pebbles. From within this bed rise the lovely, long stems of a bunch of lotus flowers. The light that is reflected from the design, showing it to such beautiful effect, seems to be a matter of chance, but there is no such thing as chance. When you are making something, whether you believe in coincidence and luck, or whether you believe – as I do – that everything has a meaning, no opportunity is to be missed.

Lotus leaves, with their lovely wavy outlines, form a second, balancing base for these beautiful flowers.

murmurings of the soul

I believe that we are here now because we were here before, and will be here again. We meet now because we existed before, and our meeting is not a matter of chance. It is as if I know you from my dreams. These are the murmurings of my soul, and in order to arouse such murmurings in yours, I have designed a flower arrangement of strange, mysterious shapes, perfect for contemplation. This is a miniature garden set in a stone tray and placed against a pale background so that the forms are clear and transparent. An anthurium leaf, the stalk of which is firmly set in florist's foam disguised by sand, provides the horizontal line. This leaf is penetrated with two stems of the pitcher plant (*Sarracenia*), a strange-looking fluted plant that seems to reach for something in the sky. Parallel until they meet in the heavens, these two stems represent an encounter between two former lives.

This miniature stone garden makes a tranquil minimalist design and creates an atmosphere that is perfect for contemplation.

the journey into emptiness

The Chinese emperor Wu-Ti, of the Liang dynasty, was a very learned scholar, steeped in the arcana of Buddhist philosophy, and when he heard, in the year 520AD, that Bodhidharma, the renowned Buddhist master, was to visit China, he was delighted. He summoned Bodhidharma to court, paid him the respect due to a great master, and asked him how much merit he would receive for all the good deeds he had done. Wu-Ti was an enlightened emperor, and he had undoubtedly done many good deeds, building schools and hospitals, looking after the elderly, giving financial support to Buddhist temples, sponsoring monks and nuns; he was what we would call an ideal monarch. In answer to his question, however, there was a pregnant pause, followed by the brusque reply, "No merit at all." Stunned, but not entirely discouraged, Wu-Ti then asked what was the essence of Buddhism, and was told, "No essence at all." Finally, his patience at breaking point, Wu-Ti asked Bodhidharma for his identity: "Well, then, who is he that is talking with me now?" He received the reply, "I do not

know." Bodhidharma, having been thrown out of court, went to the Shao-Lin monastery and sat cross-legged in front of a wall, where he remained for the next nine years, practising *pi-kuan,* or "wall-contemplation". Was he waiting for someone to get the true message of Buddhism, or was he staring deep into the darkness of his own soul? I do not think that he would have told us. Here is my small tribute to Bodhidharma, a man of principle. My emblem of his journey into emptiness is made of dried leaves, standing in an Asian bowl made of paper and wood. These are given definition by white, partly dried lotus (*Nelumbo*) flowers. The whole arrangement is set on a brown surface.

Dried lotus flower (*Nelumbo*)

Ball of string on bamboo box

An atmosphere of calmness is created by these partly dried lotus flowers and the antique colouring of the other objects.

time to cleanse
the soul

There comes a time when it is necessary to stop and think, to reconsider the past, assess the present and start again. This is when the soul is cleansed. This arrangement is designed as an aid to meditation. It is distinctly Japanese in that emphasis is laid on straight lines, playing with them in order to create variety. Down the middle of the rectangular table is a phormium leaf. This is crossed with two strelitzia leaves to create a visual tension. Sempervivums provide an accent, and a white stone dish highlights the focal point of tension.

A dish of grey-white stone draws attention to the focal point of the design. All the lines leading from this point are different.

the mind balance

This aid to meditation was made with quietness in mind and it is therefore quite symmetrical. Sempervivums come in many delicate shades; the ones in this design are dark green and purple, with gentle touches of red. The plants are placed in three dark wax bowls, set in a straight line along the centre of the table. Grey-white stone dishes under the bowls temper the earthy colours of the plants. Such colours are ideal for the creation of a quiet atmosphere, an ambience suitable for relaxation, deep thought and reconsideration of the future.

Earthy colours set in light surroundings provide points of focus, objects of meditation. Gentle colours, simplicity and symmetry are the basic elements of this design.

a garden of healing

The training methods of Zen are based on *zazen*, which means sitting in meditation in order to expel impure thoughts and achieve spiritual enlightenment, or *satori*. Every pilgrim searches for this in his or her own way, but it is recognized that the processes of rational thought, useful as they are in so many ways, are of limited help in the quest for *satori*, which is more likely to be discovered through direct intuition. As you seek the flashes of inspiration that will quell anxiety and calm your mind, you need to be in touch with the reality of the universe. You need a mirror for your soul. The Zen garden is the universe in microcosm. In order to emancipate yourself, you do not need to dominate the world; you do not need to own a mansion; all you need is a small room, with a roof that does not leak and sufficient food to still the pangs of hunger. In this room, you can make a tiny Zen garden, and when you have one, then everything, including spiritual freedom, becomes possible. Enlightenment is to be found within yourself.

You will need
- **4 squares of black slate**
- **white pebbles**
- **small grey pebbles**
- **3 stones**
- **scissors**
- **bun moss**
- **sweet chestnuts in their husks**

1

2

3

4

1 Prepare four black slates and arrange them in a square.

2 Spread white pebbles on the square and form them into an island.

3 Place three well-chosen stones at strategic points within your "island". The placement of these stones is most important, as the distances between them will either create a sense of disturbance or the sense of balance that you require. Even such a simple task requires aesthetic sensibility.

4 Arrange the bun moss around the stones and add a number of chestnuts to look like vegetation. Add some small, grey pebbles near one of the stones. Sprinkle with imagination and the elements of the universe are yours to contemplate.

a forest of
the mind

Even if the forest of your mind has been burnt to a cinder, because you have suffered something terrible and lost your faith and confidence, survive it and new life will begin to stir. The spirit is amazingly resilient, and people survive the apparently impossible, without ever knowing how they did it. This arrangement is a celebration of those who survive suffering. The burnt forest is represented by a stack of charcoal, the rebirth of hope by a beautiful cream dahlia. Because the charcoal is horizontal, and I wanted only the head of the cream dahlia to appear, a vertical line was necessary, so I used a modernist depiction of a woman, curved and graceful, to stand for the spirit of goodwill. She rises like a phoenix from the ashes of despair and makes her healing gesture of hope. It is important that this vertical accent is dark, because nothing should detract from the brilliance of the flower.

A background the colour of a clear blue sky sets off to perfection this combination of forms and colours.

ripe silence

You shouldn't try to do this or that.

It just is, so let it be.

My daily activities are not different,

Only I am naturally in harmony with them.

Taking nothing, renouncing nothing,

in every circumstance no hindrance, no conflict...

Drawing water, carrying firewood,

This is supernatural power, this marvellous activity.

(Zen Philosophy, Zen Practice)

suppliers

Harumi Nishi can be contacted at the
Lilies-of-the-Valley Flower School/Flower Shop
(H.N. Flower School by Harumi Nishi):

Osaka, Japan
Kyoritsu Building 4F 1-16-17
Higashishinsaibashi Chuo-ku
Osaka 542-0083 Japan
Tel/Fax (81) 6 6243 0023
Nagoya, Japan
405 Eguchi-Haitsu 5-13-27
Sakae Naka-ku Nagoya-shi
Aichi 460 0008 Japan
Tel (81) 52 251 0043
http://www.hnflowers.com
email info@hnflowers.com

UNITED KINGDOM
Flowers
Liberty plc
Regent's Street
London W1R 6AH
Tel 020 7734 1234

Jane Packer Flowers
56 James Street
London W1 8BU
Tel 020 7935 2673 Fax 020 7486 1300

Paula Pryke Flowers
20 Penton Street
London N1 9PS
Tel 020 7837 7336
Fax 020 7837 6766
Email paula@paula-pryke-flowers.com

Accessories
Anna French
343 King's Road
London SW3 5ES
Tel 020 7351 1126

Borovick Fabrics
16 Berwick Street
London W1V 4HP
Tel 020 7437 2180

B&Q Nationwide
Enquiries 0800 444840
General DIY superstore

The Conran Shop
Michelin House
81 Fulham Road
London SW3 6RD
Tel 020 7727 0707
*Classic furniture and stylish
home accessories*

Function
1st Floor
12 Greatorex Street
London E1 5NF
Tel 020 7792 1988
*A selection of simple furniture
and accessories*

Gong
182 Portobello Road
London W11 2EB
Tel 020 7565 4162
*Furniture, bamboo benches, wall hangings,
reed mats and ceramics from China and
Far East*

Kara Kara
2a Pond Place
London SW3 6QJ
Tel 020 7591 0891
*Selection of furniture, ceramics, fabrics, bamboos
screens and benches from the Far East*

Michael Reeves Interiors
91a Pelham Street
London SW7 2NJ
Tel 020 7225 2501 Fax 020 7225 3060
*Classic, simple, dark wood furniture, stone top
tables with a hint of the Far East*

Neal Street East
5 Neal Street
Covent Garden
London WC2H 9PU
Tel 020 7240 0135
*Accessories from the Far East: fans, kimonos,
ceramics, silk and sari cushions*

Twelve
Mail order: 020 7686 0773
Benches, incense blocks and accessories

UNITED STATES

Flowers

Florida Plants

Online Garden Store

www.floridaplants.com

Tel (888) 284-5153

Garden materials and plants

Accessories

Earth Spirit

4343 16th Street #117

Moline, IL 61265

Tel (877) 918-0627 Fax: (309) 736-0688

www.earthspirits.net

Home furnishings and accessories

Go East

1304 Logan Street, Suite K

Costa Mesa, CA 92626

Tel (714)668-1296 Fax (714)668-1297

www.goeastinc.com

Home furnishings and accessories

Pier 1 Imports

Tel (800) 245-4595

www.pier1.com

Call or check online for store locations

furniture and home accessories

AUSTRALIA AND NEW ZEALAND

Flowers

Flower of Zen

222a Glenmore Road

Paddington, NSW 2021

Tel 612 9380 2722

Flowers by Special Arrangement

116 Carlton Gore Road

Newmarket, Auckland

Tel (09) 524 0042

Flower Temple

98-100 Station Street

Fairfield, NSW VIC 3078

Tel 613 9482 7999

Accessories

Bones, Stones & Harmony

202 King Street

Pukehole

Auckland

Tel (09) 238 5777

Made in Japan

20 Rokeby Road

Subiaco

WA 6008

Tel 618 9388 2666

Urban Homewares

628 Darling Street

Rozelle, NSW 2039

glossary

bana, flower

bassara, novelty

bi, beauty

bodhimanda, sacred place where Shakyamuni Buddha found enlightenment

Buddha, awakened (Siddhartha Gautama became awakened to truth and was thereafter known as the Buddha); the spiritual founder of Buddhism; anyone who has achieved perfect enlightenment

Buddha nature, one's original nature; universal nature; the true nature of what really is

chozubachi, stone hand-basin

doh, movement

Esoteric Buddhism, the form of Buddhism originally imported from China

haiku, three-line poem of 17 syllables

hakkai, the eight rough seas

ikebana, Japanese art of flower arranging

iki, stylishness

kami, nature spirits; the gods of the *shinto* religion

kensho, first step on the path to enlightenment

ketsu, conclusion

ki, introduction

koan, philosophical conundrum

la, attainment

ma, distance

manda, essence

mandala, graphic aid to meditation

mandara, Japanese version of the mandala

mantras, verbal rituals

Manyoshu, anthology of ancient poems

mu, nothingness

mudras, bodily rituals

mushin, state of mental emptiness achieved through meditation

nageire, informal flower arranging

nirvana, final release from cycle of rebirth

noh, drama

rikka, flower arrangement that is standing or erect

Rinzai school of Zen Buddhism, Eisai (1141–1215) introduced the Rinzai sect

sabi, the beauty of antiquity

sake, alcoholic drink brewed from fermented rice

samsara, the cycle of rebirth

satori, enlightenment

sei, stillness

seiden, Chinese style of dividing land into different parts

seika, "cut flowers", arranged as if living

sengyokukan, landscape that looks particularly beautiful in autumn

Shinto, ancient religion of Japan; indigenous Japanese religion

sho, development

Soto school of Zen Buddhism, Dogen (1200–53) introduced the Soto sect

Sukiya, pared-down style of domestic architecture; style used in teahouses

tatami, mat

ten, turn

tokonoma, alcove or domestic altar

tsukubai, tearoom washbasin

wabi, concept of simplicity: less is better

wabi sabi, antique grace and refinement

zazen, meditation

index

Page numbers in *italics* refer to illustrations.

Acknowledgements

Author's Acknowledgements
I would like to give very special thanks to my editor, Caroline Davison, for her help and encouragement throughout the course of this project. The same goes for the photographers, James Mitchell and Norio Asai, who took these stunning photographs and showed endless patience while doing so. A special thank you is also due to Juliana Leite-Goad.

I am very grateful to J.M. François, who interpreted my thoughts and reconstructed my English throughout most of the text; to Alyn Bailey for his invaluable help and vital contribution to the Introduction; and to Alan Higgs who has encouraged me in my career.

Of course, I would also like to offer heartfelt thanks to my best friends and colleagues: Hiromi Wada, Kinuyo Matsumoto, Masayo Yamada, Hideko Isaka, Hiromi Nakao, Yuko Nakatani, Mineko Nishida, Naoko Sakai, Eri Matsushima, Kazuno Yamada, Sumiko Baba and Ayako Watanabe.

Thanks are also due to gkn.net and their secure Global Private Network product.

Last, but certainly not least, I would like to thank the members of my family, to whom I am eternally grateful.

Publisher's Acknowledgements
The publishers would like to thank the following institutions in Japan for allowing photography to take place on their premises: Tofuku-ji; Ryoan-ji; The Miyako (Keage Sanjo, Kyoto 605-0052, Japan); Kaikohen; S x L Corporation; Tsuki no Hana; Youshuen; Sakura-ya; Arakawa.

The publishers would also like to thank the following for lending accessories and furniture for photography: Aero, Arc Gallery, Benetton Paints, C.X.V. Furniture, The Conran Shop, David Wainwright, Function Design, Gong, Kara Kara, Michael Reeves Interiors, Ming Mang, Muji, Neal Street East, Opium, Snap Dragon and Twelve.

All the photographs in this book were taken by James Mitchell, except for the following:
KEY: l = left r = right b = bottom t = top

Norio Asai 30 (left); 31 (both); 32-33 (all); 34-35 (all); 36–37 (all); 40; 44–45 (all); 46–47 (all); 54; 55; 82; 87bl; 114; 142bl; 143; 144; 153; 158 (bl); endpaper. **Harumi Nishi** 10-11; 30 (right); 41; 69; 72br; 75; 78; 83; 88; 96; 97; 100 (both); 110; 111; 115t; 125; 128tr; 129 (both); 142tr; 156bl; 160.